# Roadway of Family Memories Cripple Creek, Virginia

A Journey in time through the hills of Virginia

Wayne and Hattie King

# Roadway of Family Memories

# Cripple Creek, Virginia

# Wayne and Hattie King

WHK Publishing Company
1909 Regal Avenue
Medford, OR 97501
Copyright 2009
Revised 2013

ISBN: 978-0-9826796-0-9

**All rights reserved.** No part of this book may be reproduced or transmitted in any form or by any means, electronic or mechanical, including photocopying, recording or by any information storage and retrieval system without written permission from the author. Exceptions are made for brief excerpts to be used in published reviews.

Printed in the United States of America

# Acknowledgments

Many people were so very kind, helping me compile this book regarding my childhood days in Cripple Creek, Virginia. With all the telephone calls, pictures, newspaper reports, clippings, e-mails, personal conversations, mailings and shipping, I pray I haven't omitted someone. If I have, please accept my apology and deep gratitude and appreciation for your help.

A special thanks to my wife, Hattie May King, for her encouragement and to my first cousin Pamela (King) Wiggins living in Franklin, Virginia for her encouragement too, as well as my Uncle Keister King in Virginia Beach for his humorous attitude and encouragement as well.

I'm so appreciative for my wife, Hattie May King for proofing so many of my first writings and making suggestions for more descriptive details in the stories. Others who assisted in the proof reading are as follows: Bob and Barbara Porter, Ruth Davidson, Betty Nucholls, Linda O' Daniel, Dusty Armstrong. Others who assisted in procuring tangible items, special research in the archives of Wythe County, Virginia and Rockingham County, North Carolina. Wythe County Historical Society, Clayta Bryant, Town of Wytheville, Department of Museums, Jeanette Wood, Marcella C. Taylor, Administrative/Marketing Assistant, Pearl C. Woods, Cecilia Merritt, Bill Kittrell, Commonwealth of Virginia, Department of Game and Inland Fisheries, Richmond, Virginia, Jeffery Simmons, Nate Hubbard, Wytheville Enterprises, Leanin' Tree, "Wrong Number" by Nate Owens, Dairy Antiques, Paul and Linda, Daphne Rosenbaum, Freddie Rosenbaum, Debbie Richardson, Eddie Yoncy, Frances Yoncy, C. Bayne Grubb, R.K. Grubb, Donna L. Cook, Carlene Sandhagen, Buddy Griffin, Carl and Keitsie Anderson. A special thanks to Roxy Hamel for her positive support with transcribing my text into the computer, and for the help by Matthew Jenkins with his technical ability and support. Also, special thanks to the children who listened to many of the stories over time. Jessica, Jeremiah, Joseph and Jonathon Armstrong.

Scripture quotations in this book are from the following source. The World Publishing Company, The King James Version of the Holy Bible, (KJV). The Text conformable to that of the edition of 1611, commonly known as the authorized or King James Version.

# Table of Contents

Acknowledgements................................................................... 5

Introduction............................................................................ 11
(Short Stories Written About My Childhood)

Family Stories........................................................................ 13

Cripple Creek, Virginia.......................................................... 17

Exciting Bus Ride and Lunch With Grandmother..................... 19

Wytheville, Virginia............................................................... 33

Bus Routes From Cripple Creek to Fries and on Occasions to Wytheville
    (A story told by Robert Porter, Cripple Creek, Virginia)............... 35

Grandmother's Bakery............................................................ 39

Cherry Pies............................................................................ 41

Daddy Gene's Pipe and The Holy Bible................................... 43

Daddy Gene's Strange Behavior.............................................. 45
    (Filled With The Holy Spirit)

The Deer Chase...................................................................... 47

Catfishing in the Old Francis Mill Creek.................................. 49

Colored Rocks in the old Mill Creek........................................ 51
    (Young geologists)

Hog Killing Time................................................................... 53

Five Gallon Lard Cans Full of Silver Coins............................. 57

The Old Greasy Pole.................................................................. 59
    (Dark Cave or Piper's Cave)

The Old Straw Tick Mattress Bed and the Chicken Feather Pillow......... 61

Refreshing "Spring Water" After Church.................................... 63

The Hawkbill Knife.................................................................. 67

Mrs. Davidson's Home in Cripple Creek, Virginia....................... 69

Dedication: Special Tribute to my friend Nathaniel Sidney Davidson, Captain U.S. Army.................................................................. 73

Friends.................................................................................... 96

Artifacts in the Garden............................................................. 97

A Day of Antiquing with my Dad, Dillard King......................... 99

The Old Schoolhouse in Cripple Creek, Virginia....................... 111
    (Miss Peggy Allison)

Time For Recess.....................................................................113
    (Miss Peggy Allison)

Quiet Time "Lights Out"........................................................115

Grandmother's Old Churn-Homemade Butter........................117

Crockett's General Store and The Old Telephone.....................121

Information Please................................................................. 123

Reflections.............................................................................125

Doctor Andrew Bayne Grubb, a Visit to Grandmother's.........127

A Sunrise Service in Cripple Creek........................................ 133

Slop Jars and Chamber Pots..................................................139

The Old Springhouse............................................................. 141

Cripple Creek's U.S. Post Office............................................. 143

Grandmother King and a Buried Treasure................................159
    (Spanish Mill Coin 1784)

Hands in the Cookie Jar......................................................... 163

Hattie's Kitchen..................................................................... 165

Are All the Children In?......................................................... 167

There's a Real Change In Cripple Creek................................. 171

The Old Water Pump............................................................. 173

Forever Giving--Forever Living............................................. 175

Time to Say Good-Bye to Old Cripple Creek..........................177

In Loving Memory of Keister Troy King
    (His Pontoon Boat Vanishes over the horizon)....................... 179

Celebration of Life................................................................. 181

# Introduction

## Short Stories Written About My Childhood

Short stories written about my childhood in Cripple Creek, Virginia are those cherished about my step-grandfather and grandmother, other family members, friends and neighbors living in the surrounding area. It is only by the grace of God I live today to share them with you as so many times my thoughts have returned to the corners of my mind only to reflect upon the many times spent in the mountains and valleys and in the wonderful church just above an artesian well or spring near the church just across the old wagon bridge from Cripple Creek.

With joy and praise I give all glory and thanks to our Father in heaven for His love, and grace, dedicating this book to my wife, Hattie King and our children, Timothy King, Belynnda (King) Metzler, John King (deceased) and the many friends and neighbors who made it possible in collecting information necessary for this short book.

Wayne King

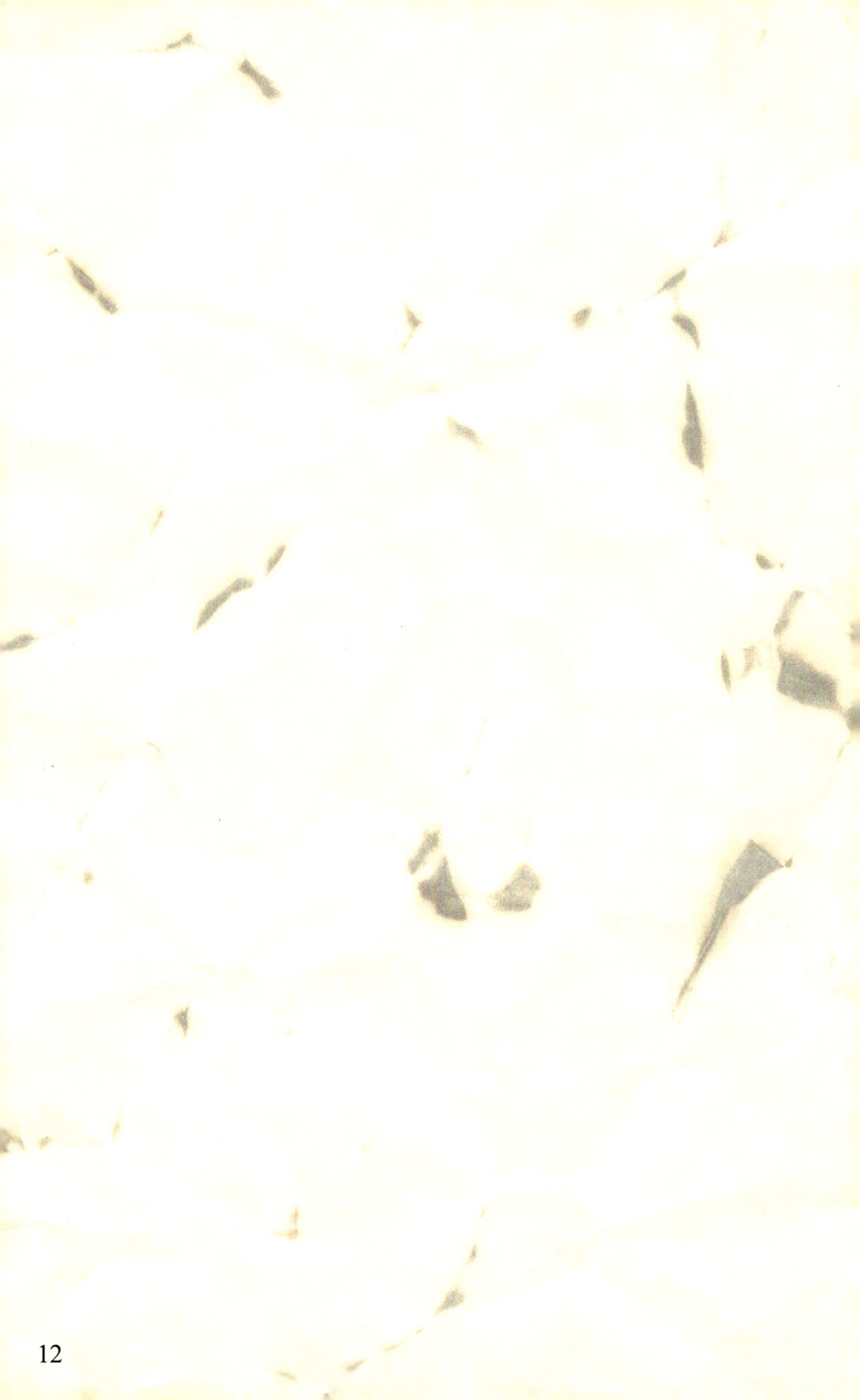

# Family Stories

Why is it important to share stories with our children and grandchildren? Isn't television, computers, cell phones, electronic devices and other high tech gadgets enough to entertain the minds of our youth? Are we becoming a society without books? I sure hope not. Without question technology has its place in our world but not at the expense of robbing the formable and brilliant minds of our youth.

Some time ago Mary Pipher wrote a book, "The Shelter of Each Other." She gave some very interesting advice. In her story she gives the advice to troubled families and what they must do to rebuild the continuity between the older and younger generations. We are living in a technological society where in many cases children overuse the TV, video games and other devices. When uncles, aunts, grandparents visit their homes, children are sent to another room to indulge their minds in the technological world excluding the past stories and conservations by their relatives. The children never hear many of the experiences the older generations have endured. Children need to hear these stories. I hope by writing a few about my life and living in Cripple Creek, Virginia will encourage some or all to think about what we're about to lose. If we as an older generation don't share our lives and stories with our younger generation, what will become of the next one?

Maybe we need to set reminders somewhere before us, as did the Israelites in the Old Testament. Throughout the Old Testament there was a high value placed on teaching the younger generations their spiritual heritage.

While living in Cripple Creek and attending Sunday school and church, my teacher taught many flannelgraph Bible stories. I can't say for sure if the following story was among the stories, but I do remember the story in the Book of Joshua 4:6-7. After the waters of the Jordan River were parted, the priest crossed on dry ground and God commanded there be twelve stones removed from the midst of the river and placed on dry ground on the other side to be a memorial for future generations. "That this may be a sign among you, that when your children as their fathers in time to come, saying, what mean ye by these stones? Then ye shall answer them, that the waters of the Jordan were cut off before the ark of the covenant of the Lord...."

It's extremely important and imperative we teach and train our children to have a good value system as they grow and develop their own set of values. As they look back to their childhood days, they can say I'm proud of what I was taught as a child growing up.

As a retired Public School Teacher from California, I've witnessed time after time the heartbreak of children coming to me at the Middle School Level, weeping because they felt the hurt from home as their parents didn't care about them. It's when a little girl comes to you on the playground with open arms asking as they reach out for you, "Will you be my daddy today?" or, a young boy honors you with a note saying, "You've been my dad this year in school. Thanks for all your caring and love." On another occasion, a little boy said to my wife, "Will you be my grandmother? Or, will you go away as all the others have."

My wife and I received a number of children running away from their homes to our home thinking their parents had rejected them, and we would make contact with their parents. On one occasion, the mother said regarding her daughter, " She came to you, so you keep her." What a real heartbreak this was.

Years passed and this same young girl returned to us with a heart of appreciation and gratitude, explaining she was able to complete high school and married a young man and had started a family. We were elated she returned, sharing her story and keeping us informed and explaining to us, as she said, "There is still hope for me." She was so excited about life and that she had a second chance doing the right things.

May we find ways to love, teach and train our children and others as well, to share their lives together as families. May we reach out with open arms as God does for us to the lonely, hurting generations, My wife and I did to a very young girl sitting on a railroad track in Ashland, Oregon, on one very, very foggy day. Heartbroken, tears flowing, a stranger, rejected yet willing to listen to my wife as arms reached out to each other. We were so happy she wasn't killed as she walked away with a smile, returning to her dwelling and feeling she wasn't forgotten and believing there is still God's true love in a confused world.

# Stories About Cripple Creek And Surrounding Areas of Virginia From About 1944

# Cripple Creek, Virginia

A view of a quiet little village called Cripple Creek tucked away in the hills and mountains of Virginia with all its eloquent beauty and majestic surroundings, flooding into one's eyes and all corners of your mind.

Suddenly a door swings open within your thoughts as you listen to the hush of love, joy and peace engulfing your soul in silence and wrapping you with eternal thoughts, irreplaceable, that only God understands with all the spiritual groans from within.

Above view of Cripple Creek near a reservoir.
Date of picture unknown.

Grandmother and step-grandfather's home as seen from across Francis Mill Creek.
Photo courtesy Donna Lou Cook 1953

Mr. and Mrs. E.H. Worrell
(Daddy Gene and grandmother)

Grandmother Worrell
Date of pictures unknown.

# Exciting Bus Ride and Lunch With Grandmother

I can't wait for Saturday to arrive! You see Saturday at grandmother's was very special and filled with excitement!

Grandmother's home was nestled in the beautiful Blue Ridge Mountains of Southern Virginia, in a little village called Cripple Creek. A slow lazy stream of water named Francis Mill Creek, meandered from the mountains through the misty valleys, passing directly in front of grandmother's home and through the little village.

Saturday morning was a time of peace and tranquility, filled with excitement, bliss and God's love. It was time for just grandmother and I to spend the day together, boarding an old bus to journey to a small town (Wytheville, Virginia) some ten to fifteen miles away. You see grandmother didn't own a car, and never had a license to drive.

With excitement and a heart filled with anticipation, grandmother and I boarded the old country bus, which was dilapidated and somewhat uncomfortable with its rigid seats and filled with dust from the old dirt roads. Yet even with the shifting and grinding sound of the gears clanging, the driver tried his best to make our trip a pleasant one. He was a wonderful gentleman and so very polite to all the passengers. He would tip his hat and say, "Good morning!" and give each a wonderful smile to bless their day.

As we departed grandmother's little home and headed toward the town of Wytheville, we first passed by the old sycamore tree and wood structured bridge, crossing over the small Francis Mill Creek just beyond grandmother's home. The old sycamore tree was my favorite as it stood so strong and majestic, so noble and stately with its mottled appearance, having an age of many years. Its bark would peel off in large brown rough textured sheets, leaving a cream colored fresh bark beneath. Her leaves were shaped almost like a heart, with three to five lobes, very thick with a light green in color and feeling hairy beneath the leaf. It was an expression to me of the love God has for us, so strong, so beautiful and so awesome. And along with all its beauty the fruit formed in a string of three or four balls, so attractive in its spherical design, being brown in color, yielding a prickly texture to ones touch…such a creation by God.

Then there was the old bridge stretched across the little creek, with just enough room for a person to walk. It was always so exciting to watch the water flowing below and watch the foam from the whirlpools move around and around. The bridge had two strong tree logs supporting the narrow planks nailed on top of the logs with a handrail above on one side to help keep someone from falling into the creek. It was fun to run and bounce on the little bridge just to watch it sway and go up and down. It is a wonder we didn't fall into the creek.

Picture taken from grandmother's home looking toward Mrs. Henley's home. The old shed near the sycamore tree was the bus stop (N.J. Wright's bus) for Wytheville and the wood bridge crossing Francis Mill Creek to Mrs. Henley's home was used many times as a play area. We ran back and forth making the bridge bounce up and down for fun. Sure happy it didn't collapse. Look very close for the bridge handrail for the bridge starting beside the old shed. It was constructed of logs and planks. "Wonderful days!"

As we continued our journey along the creek, to one side of the road was Mrs. Henley's home . She had so many chickens and always so many beautiful brown eggs for sale, and many times she had little bannie hen eggs, too. They were so small and looked like bird eggs. Sometimes grandmother would send me over to Mrs. Henley's home to buy her eggs.

Mrs. Henley's old home where I once purchased eggs for my grandmother in the 1940's.

Mrs. Hattie King
Wife

Pictures January 1993

Also, we would pass by the home where Mr. Reeve's daughter, Betty, lived, and had her beauty salon across the street and stilted over the old Mill Creek that runs in front of grandmother's home and Mrs. Henley's place. What an unusual salon it was. So here it is in her own words, as Betty describes her little shop. "I started a beauty shop back in the seventies. We owned this store building (Rustic looking) and I had a shop in one end of it. I had one shampoo basin and a chair, a sturdy shelf up over the basin. I had a large galvanized bucket. We put a hole down at the bottom, and put a spicket in it and a rubber hose. I lived across the road from the building and I carried my hot and cold water. I also had one dryer and chair, one oil stove, one dressing table and chair, and one table to work from, and, two large mirrors on two walls. I worked with a lot of elderly people and I didn't charge too much. It worked well and customers seemed to be pleased." What a strange, yet ingenious setup this was. Grandmother always enjoyed having Betty do her hair. In the early seventies my wife Hattie had Betty do up her hair and it was a great pleasure watching her. One thing for sure, Betty is a wonderful person (lives in Roanoke, Virginia) and always displays a sweet and personable attitude. She was always smiling and had a very positive outlook anytime I ever spoke with her. She loves people, and her mother was the same way, she always wanted me to see her agate ring when I visited her as a young boy.

Betty Nucholls's Home

My mother Francis Juanita King and Betty Nucholls and son,
Edwin S. Nucholls.

Special picture of Betty Nucholls.
Photo October 1957

Betty Nucholls's Rustic Beauty Shop

Back view of Betty's Beauty Shop

View underneath Betty's Beauty Shop and a quartz rock from the ground.
Pictures January 1993

Guess we better get on down the road to have lunch with grandmother. Soon, we were passing by Mr. Kirby's home and old country store. It was a very small little store with one front door and two small windows, one on each side of the door. Mr. Kirby always let me come in to see all the candies inside this beautiful glass case. Inside the candy case, which was filled with so many beautiful rainbow colored candies, I would just stand there motionless staring into the long glass candy case as Mr. Kirby dragged his one leg along the old wooden floor…as you see he was disabled and couldn't move too fast, maybe from a stroke. Then my mouth would start to water, I could just taste the juicy and most delicious sweetness of each piece of candy as the smell, the fragrance, the pleasant sensations filled my nose, and my stomach would start to churn as milk making butter. My whole body was aroused with each sensation of the sparkles of light bouncing off from those beautiful pieces of candy…my body made music to every fiber in my chilled arms.

Mr. Kirby was so very polite and would ask, "How is your grandmother doing?" "Is she ailing or feeling better?" I would just say, "Okay except for her arthritis, she's doing fine." Sometimes he would offer me a piece of those beautiful pieces of candy, and that was so nice of him. I would always say, "Thank you Mr. Kirby!" Then I would be on my way. Just one more thought though. Mr. Kirby's wife Bessie, would say to me, during apple season, "Would you like some fresh and delicious apples from our tree in the front yard?" My answer was always yes, and thanks! Grandmother loved Mrs. Kirby's apples for her wonderful apple pies. More stories to follow.

Mr. and Mrs. Kirby's home restored.

Note the roof, building on the right in the picture.

The sign reads, "Buddy's Place."
Years ago, it was Kirby's Store.
Pictures January 1993

Soon we were passing Mrs. Macia Davidson's beautiful home . It was a big tall two- story place with a huge yard and grape vines meandering along the two upper and lower porches. The winding courses of the vines were as a stream of water forming an ornamental pattern, a crisscrossing over and through each spindle of the porches. The ornate and elaborately designed structure with supporting Doric Columns and brick pillars was a fascinating sight to behold…such beauty and a place of comfort and shade.

Mrs. Macia Davidson was such a wonderful person and always a delight. Her son, Nathaniel, "Nat," was my best friend in Cripple Creek. When visiting, she would say to me, "Wayne, please come in", and, "are you hungry?" "Be seated", and, "how are your grandmother and step-daddy, Gene, doing?" Before answering, and in my mind, I would think of how she suffered from arthritis and how painful it was for her. Then as she served me with kindness and never a harsh word, I would express an appreciation for her generous hospitality and politely answer her questions regarding my grandparents. A very special lady.

Mrs. Macia Davidson's home.

Better get going because we'll soon be into the center of the little village of Cripple Creek. As we continued down the road we would soon pass the old Crockett General Store. It too was stilted over the old Francis Mill Creek as were so many other stores and homes. Inside the store one would find the old wood floors and a big black potbellied stove standing in a sandbox of about five feet square. Here, many village folks, mostly men, would come in the evening to be sociable, just enjoying the company of others, sharing their fascinating tails or stories and using the sandbox to spit their yucky and terrible snuff and tobacco juices into. The smell was enough to make one sick. However, the store was filled with friendship and love to care and help each other, especially in hard times, because this was during a time of World War II, and many people didn't have much, but they shared what they did have. I was enthralled by the glass showcases, filled with sewing items, clothing, candies, foods, tools and many other fascinating objects. One thing that really caught my eye was the old ring box telephone hanging on the wall. I fell in love with this old phone. It was about eighteen inches long with two large black bells on the top face. Along with the bells was the mouth piece and a note pad surface for writing. On the right side there was a hand crank for sending out electrical signals, and a receiver on the left side for hearing the human voices so far away. What a beautiful old oak phone box. More stories to follow.

Crockett Grocery Store, presently owned by Mr. and Mrs. Yonce. Picture January 1993

We must be about our journey, and get down the road. Soon we approached the old U.S. Post Office and gas station. People in Cripple Creek didn't have mailboxes in front of their homes. They were assigned a post office box in the Post Office and each day people would pick up their mail. It was a real treat for me to pick up the mail for my grandmother because I so enjoyed using the combination process of characters to open the mailbox. You had to turn the knob one way then another until you heard the click of the tumblers and the alignment of the combination. Then the little brass door on the box would open. A later story will explain in detail, more about the U.S. Post Office.

On down the road we went across a small metal bridge just before the old church I attended with my grandmother and step-grandfather, Daddy Gene. My Sunday school teacher used the old flannel graph boards to teach the stories about the Holy Bible. It was very exciting to watch how each character and objects clung to the flannel graph board as my teacher explained each Biblical story and required all students to memorize Bible verses each week for class. During the warm months after church, I would scurry down the side of the hill adjacent to the church property to a very beautiful artesian spring. It was so big and the water bubbled up so fast and crystal clear. The spring was awesome as huge rocks were all around the spring with green moss hanging from the tree limbs and the cold water was so pure. As I bent face down and touched my lips to the cold water I could see my face reflecting back at me and little creatures below smiling as to say, "Hello, welcome to our home." What an experience God provided for such a young boy as I. Another story to follow about church.

Before arriving at the Cripple Creek School building, we must mention the old Beverly Mill where there was once a swinging bridge leading across Cripple Creek to the mill. I seldom went to the old mill but it was always fun to watch the old waterwheel turn.

The next point along our way was the old white schoolhouse. The school was so small and set some distance from the main road. Our teacher Miss Peggy Allison was a young and very beautiful and nice teacher. She taught three grade levels in one single classroom. The first row was first grade, second row second grade and third row third grade. The room was so nice and we had inkwells made into our desks. We had to dip our pens into the inkwells and practice our handwriting every single day. It was practice, practice and more practice. It was extremely important to have good handwriting. Windows surrounded us and in the winter months it was so wonderful to fire up the old potbelly stove standing in the front part of the classroom. It was my responsibility to go outside and bring in the coal for the fire. It was so cold at times, especially when it snowed…but we all had so much fun at recess and lunch as we were permitted to bring our sleds for the hills covered with snow. The toboggans were fun too.

Just in case you are wondering about the restrooms, we didn't have any…just the Johnny house. Girls to the left of the classroom and boys to the right…now you know. More stories to follow.

Anyway, down the road we go, over the magnificent rolling hills of Virginia, with breath taking scenes of willow trees with snarled and twisted limbs and as one willow tree had a story behind it. This was a very huge tree and many of the mountain people had a tail or believed if you had a goiter and wanted it taken off, all you had to do is pray and the tree would take the goiter away because the tree had these huge sack like growths on it that looked like a goiter. I could never believe this story as it was just too strange for me.

As we continued down the road over one hill and then another, we soon neared the little town of Wytheville. Boy was I happy and excited to see all the big stores in town and to know that today was a very special, special day with my grandmother…to share her love and to see her smiles as we walked into the little drug store. It was about noon and grandmother and I found a nice and quiet seat, a booth where we would face each other. As the waitress approached us with a smile and with a real Southern accent, "What will it be for you two today?" I couldn't wait, so I ordered a big milkshake, and I can't remember the flavor, I just know I loved milkshakes and any would be fine. "What to eat, the waitress exclaimed?" I said, " What about you grandmother?" She said, "I'll have a milkshake too, but be sure it's not from uncontented (she really meant discontented) cows." Grandmother always reminded us of a comment she made while riding down the road one day as she saw a billboard with the words from Carnation Milk. It read, "Milk from contented cows," and she giggled and laughed because doctors told her she was in good health and nothing was wrong with her, 'except for your arthritis.' She just said, "Now I know my problem, I've been drinking milk from all those uncontented cows." The waitress laughed and her face turned red and wanted to know if we wanted anything else? Guess we'll have two bacon, lettuce and tomato sandwiches. Soon our order was ready and I was most anxious to get my teeth into that wonderful sandwich but didn't want to hurry too much, because I really enjoyed talking to grandmother. I love this kind of lunch. This was a real treat, for seldom did we have such a pleasure in town. Now for God's blessing on our food.

Grandmother and I would spend our lunch hour talking about simple things in life. We were never in a big hurry when eating. We discussed things about catching fish, looking for cherries, apples and blackberries in Cripple Creek, and how we would help each other, we laughed at funny stories about the old slop jar in the closet used in the late hours of the day and night because we didn't have an inside toilet or bathroom. Soon we were on our way to buy whatever was needed-not always our wants. By late afternoon the old bus showed up and we were on our way home back to Cripple Creek. We were tired and ready for a good nights sleep on the old straw tick mattresses and feather pillows.

This brings an eventful day to a close, so full of love, smiles, hugs and memories to be cherished in one's heart forever. Spending a day with grandmother could never be replaced. She never said a hateful or harsh word to me, and always encouraged me by showing her love and giving me a place in her heart. She gave herself, her time, her patience, treating me as a special person. Just her touch to my shoulders, my face or a tender kiss told me so many things in life. She was silent at times, with not one word, but volumes poured from her inner being…I love you, you are mine, just like God's Word tells us, we are His.

It's difficult at times to reminisce the days gone by and recall the times of the simple life. Yet we must close the story for this moment of time, and look for another rainbow in the sky, a robin in a tree, or listen to the flow of water trickling over the rocks on a hillside, with a rushing wind you can't see, but talks to you as you feel the touch to your face to know of God's beauty and creation, knowing all things abound before you, sweeping your thoughts from one place to another, recalling the sunshine and friends so far and yet so near. So, may you be encouraged to love others more than yourself.

# Wytheville, Virginia

Greetings from Wytheville, Virginia

Published by Ashville Post Card Co., Ashville, N.C.

I attended George Wythe High School in 1954. After school I would head for the golf course and caddy for any of the golf players. My special and lovely homeroom teacher was Miss O' Dell at that time, and she was so strict.

I remember going to the cafeteria for lunch and students were required to sit with our homeroom teacher. No one was dismissed from the lunch table until Miss O'Dell checked your plate and then, only then, could you request to be dismissed by saying, "Miss O'Dell, may I please be excused?" If you had food on your plate, the answer was "NO!"

She was a wonderful teacher, one I'll never forget. She made an impact on my life to become a science teacher in California.

Published by Ashville Post Card Co., Ashville, N.C.
Wytheville, VA
Near Cripple Creek, VA

# Bus Routes From Cripple Creek to Fries and on Occasions to Wytheville

(A story told by Robert Porter, Cripple Creek, Virginia)

As far back as I can remember there was a bus route from Cripple Creek to Fries. It left Cripple Creek early in the morning so day shift workers could be at work by 7:00 A.M. and it returned relatively early in the afternoon because the day shift ended at 3:30 P.M..

The distance from Cripple Creek and Fries was approximately fifteen miles. The roads, early on were dirt and in winter, mud. So the life of a bus making this trip daily was relatively short.

The buses were built by the Wright family at their Black Smith's Shop. They would buy a truck chassis and build the body on the frame. There were bench seats built along the outside walls and back to back bench seats in the center. To heat the bus the exhaust pipe had been run the length of the bus under the center seats…crude but better than nothing.

N. J. Wright was the head of all this operation. He had at least four sons and I don't know of any daughters. Dewey Wright was the only one who seemed interested in carrying on the operation. The bus was usually driven by someone who worked at the Washington Mills at Fries. Those Drivers usually were connected to the Wright Family. The last long time driver, that I know of was Harold ("Cowboy") Frye, son-in-law to Dewey.

We young folk had a little Jingle we sang about Mr. Wright. It went:

" N. J. Wright a terrible sight…he runs his buses day and night."

Remember, this was an early rural setting and anyone running buses was pretty important.

Harold was called "Cowboy" because he didn't fool around. When it came time to go, he went. It was fondly said he "didn't need brakes, only a gas pedal."

On Saturdays the mill at Fries did not operate, so the bus was free to make a trip to Wytheville, usually, leaving about 10:00 A.M. and returning late afternoon or early evening. This gave people a chance to do a bit of shopping and see a movie.

I wouldn't say the operation was a huge financial success but I know Dewey Wright raised a large family off the bus line and the Black Smith Shop/Carpenter/Mechanic shop. Daddy Gene Worrell rode these buses to work for many years.

By the way, the N. in N. J. Wright stands for Nathan. He was sort of an official Lawman of some kind…perhaps a Constable or Justice of the Peace. The story told is that on his death bed and in considerable pain, that some one suggested perhaps a sip of whiskey would relieve the pain…he (Mr. Wright) reportedly said "Before you pour the Devil's dish water into me, let me do an honorable death."

Dewey Wright was the young men's Sunday School Teacher. I was a member of his class for many years. I believe him to have been a fine man.

Robert Porter<br>Mayodan NorthCarolina

Robert Porter's home place with his wife,
Barbara Ann Porter for over fifty- four years
of loving marriage.

Picture dated 1993

Madison Dewey Wright

Black Smith Shop and Bus Lines, 1929-1979.

Photos Courtesy of Helen Frye

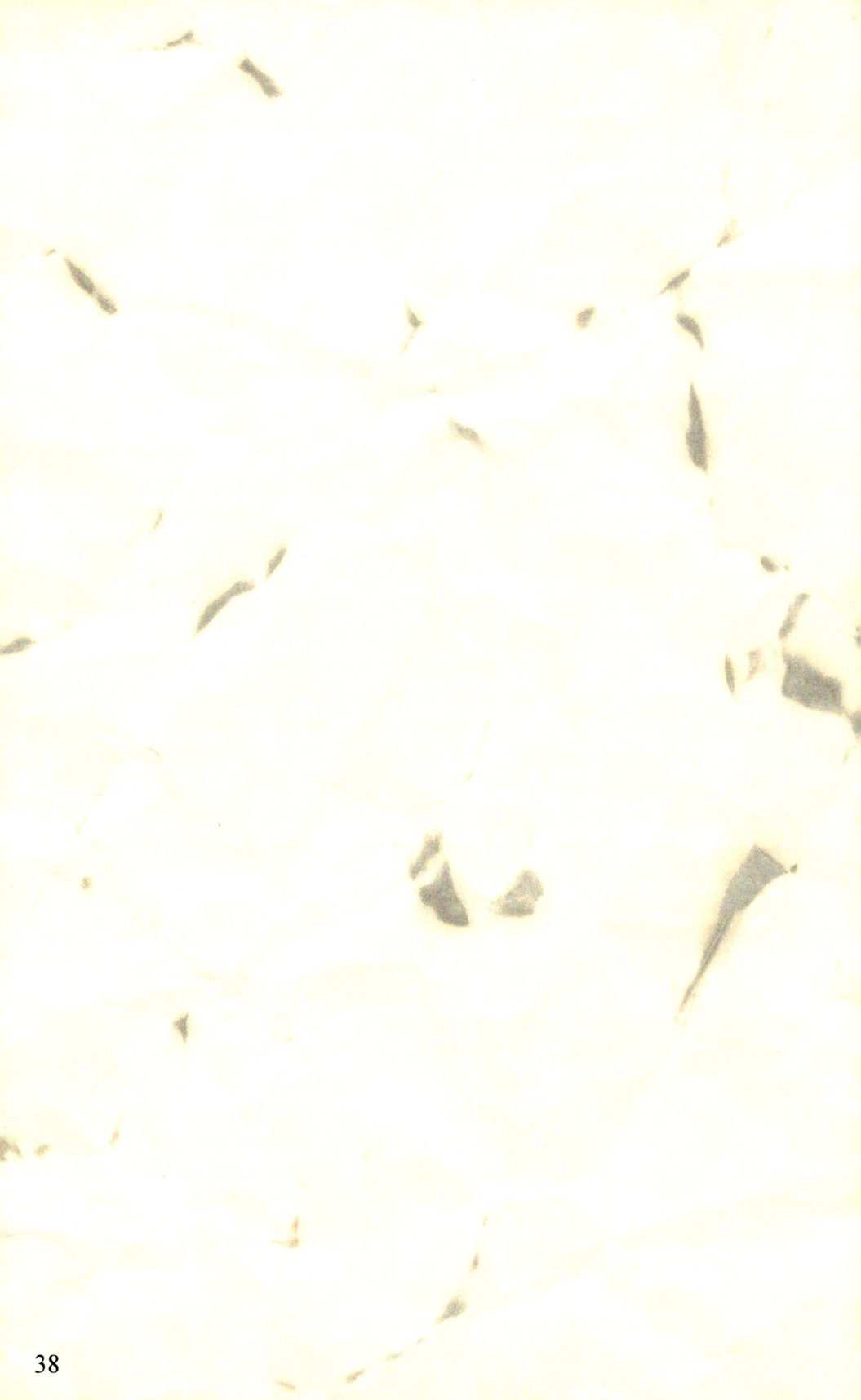

# Grandmother's Bakery

Grandmother's bakery, her kitchen, was also old fashioned and primitive and I loved it dearly. She had one of those old fashioned wood stoves with a reservoir on the right side of the stove for holding a reserve of hot water. The decoration of polished chrome over and around the warming compartment above the cooking area was so beautiful. The old oven door was decorated too. This stove was absolutely fantastic and gorgeous and would catch the eye of anyone coming into her kitchen.

The other part of her kitchen was the old flour cabinet and storage bins. It was a beautiful piece of workmanship. To the best of my knowledge, I remember it being painted a light color and with floral designs all over it. The steel shelf below that jetted out about fourteen inches, was large enough to roll out her pie dough, biscuits and the like. She stored spices and all those goodies you know, that made things taste so good and so yummy. It was fascinating to watch grandmother scurry around in her miracle kitchen and this old cabinet, singing and humming as she would say to herself, "A little pinch of this and a little dash of that is what makes it so good for anyone to taste her wares." How delightful and precious she was! Grandmother could whip up such unbelievable cakes, biscuits, muffins and the like, popping them in the oven for a given time. After baking, those gooey pans of goodies would come out so beautiful that I couldn't believe my eyes. As a young boy, it was difficult to understand how grandmother could do the impossible but she did and I loved every minute of it.

The other feature in grandmother's kitchen was the old blue and white crock, a churn with a wooden dash and cover. The cover had a hole in it for the dash to pass through, used for making butter. She always made her own butter; or shall I say when I was present, you know who was assigned to the task…yes, you guessed it…me! It was fun though. Grandmother would first prepare the milk by warming it by the old coal stove in the front room, as you see there is a special way this butter making must be done. After it was prepared, I would churn up and down with the old wood dash until the butter formed on top of the milk and grandmother would check to see if the butter was ready to be removed. Wow! My brain was really spinning in fast gear as I worked away just dreaming of how tasty my grandmother's wonderful fluffy biscuits with a slice of fresh sweet butter would taste in my mouth.   As she removed the butter, she would squeeze any excess whey from the butter and then she placed the butter in a beautiful crystal butter mold.  This was a very elegant way to present her butter in a dish and served on the table.   How beautiful things were in grandmother's kitchen.

# Cherry Pies

Grandmother would just say the words cherry pie and off I would go for a bucket and head for the hills in Virginia to find the best and largest cherries found anywhere. Of course the season for cherries had to be in for me to pick them.

As I crossed the old Mill Creek in front of grandmother's home, I always had fun bouncing on the old wooden foot bridge. It would sway back and forth and one would think it would break and fall down, but it never did. Anyway, I would scurry off bolting up the tall mountain looking for the largest cherries in the little village of Cripple Creek. Soon I would spot the largest black cherries you ever did see. They were like large marbles, and so tasty they would almost melt in your mouth. I didn't dare eat too many and find myself sick because I wanted the best cherry pie in the land, made by the best cook alive, my grandmother. I was very careful picking the cherries and tossed the bad ones for the birds to eat… don't know if they ever did.

When my bucket was full and my mouth was starting to water, I could smell and taste grandmother's pie long before she ever started the baking. I would climb down the tree, being careful not to spill the bucket of cherries for sure I didn't want to keep grandmother waiting too long for the find.

As soon as I entered the doorway, there stood grandmother with the biggest mountain smile in the whole State of Virginia. She would take the bucket of cherries and start singing and humming as she so gently washed the most beautiful cherries God had created for us. Just think, the Lord's gift to us, grandmother and I and just maybe grandpa too. She would remove the seeds from the cherries and place the cherries on the old flour, sugar and spice cabinet as she prepared to use the flour sifter and add the necessary ingredients by a little pinch of this and a little pinch of that. Soon things were in order as she used the old Maple wooden rolling pin to prepare the crust for the pie dish. "WOW!" Did grandmother know the secrets for making a cherry pie! Once everything was ready, she placed the pie in the old woodstove oven. The aroma of the pie would fill the whole house and my stomach was churning and mouth watering.

Finally, it was time to remove the pie from the oven and after our evening meal, we had our fill of the most wonderful, tasty pie in the whole State of Virginia. It would just melt in you mouth and I would thank grandmother for being the best cook ever.

# Daddy Gene's Pipe and The Holy Bible

As a young boy of about seven years, living with grandmother in Cripple Creek, Virginia, I always found it fascinating every evening to see or watch my step-grandfather sitting in his old Mission Rocking Chair, warm and comfortable in front of the old potbelly stove in the winter time, reading his Bible, smoking and puffing away on his Missouri Meerschaum's tobacco pipe, filled with Prince Albert's tobacco special and never bothering anyone, most of the time. He so enjoyed this time of the evening, rocking back and forth in his rocking chair and reading the Word of God; guess he felt relaxed and content with no more thought for the day, just reading God's Word.

This was strange and unusual to me as a young boy, seeing Daddy Gene smoking his pipe and reading the Word of God. Would God say something to him or not? Just a thought in my small little mind of that day, after all, grandmother and Daddy Gene attended the beautiful White Methodist Church just down the street by the old river. Wonder what John Wesley might have said about smoke falling from Daddy Gene's pipe on the Word of God?

Guess the old pipe smoking wasn't good for him or anyone else for that matter, but God, by His grace, gave Daddy Gene his three score and ten years, plus a few more…as he lived to be about eighty five.

Remember, be careful when you blow smoke on God's Word, because you never know what He might do.

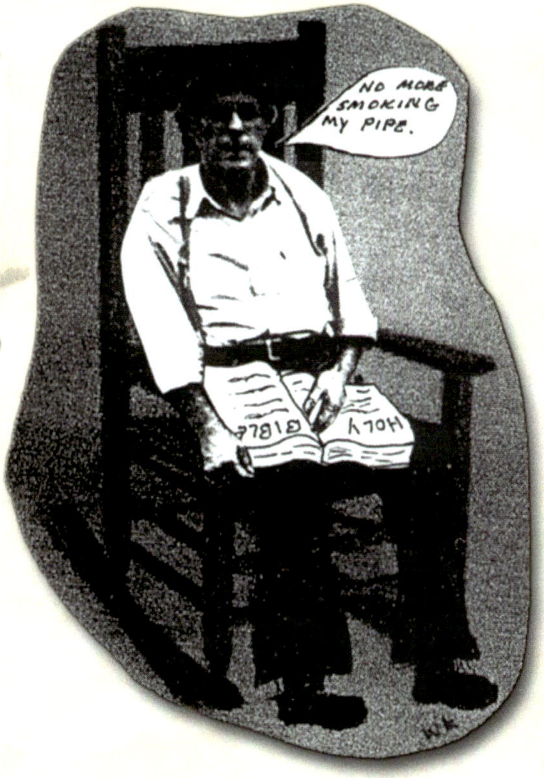
NO MORE SMOKING MY PIPE.
HOLY
BIBLE

# Daddy Gene's Strange Behavior

### (Filled With The Holy Spirit)

As it was told to me, Daddy Gene (my step-grandfather) acted very strange one very early morning (3:00 A.M.). You see, his home was constructed in such a fashion, having all rooms in the house with doors leading from one room to another in somewhat of a circle. It was said by some, he was heard running from one room to another and speaking a very strange language and shouting very loud and had his hands extended over his head praising God. To some this may sound very strange and unusual, but God does tell us in His Holy Word, "And they were filled with the Holy Ghost, and began to speak with other tongues, as the spirit gave them utterance." Acts 2:4-12 (KJV) Other references are found in I Corinthians 12:1-31. Paul the Apostle explains in I Corinthians 13:1, (KJV) "Though I speak with the tongues of men and of angels, and have not charity, I am become as sounding brass, or a tingling cymbal." Much can be said about this gift.

One thing for sure, we should never let this part of the Holy Scripture become a divisive problem to or for anyone. We should live our lives as a love letter to Jesus Christ, who lived, was crucified and rose from the dead for our sins and is willing to forgive our sins. "As far as the east is from the west, so far hath he removed our transgressions from us." Psalm 103:12 " For I will be merciful to their unrighteousness, and their sins and their iniquities will I remember no more." Hebrews 8:12 (KJV)

"For God so loved the world, that he gave his begotten Son, that whoever believeth in him should not perish, but have everlasting life." John 3:16 (KJV)

God is the same yesterday, today and forever…"Jesus Christ the same yesterday, and today, and for ever." Hebrews 13:8 (KJV)

Just as I came to the foot of the cross, it all started in Cripple Creek, Virginia in the little church by Cripple Creek where there was a spring of living water bubbling up from the ground which gave me more understanding about what Jesus said, "…but the water that I give him shall be in him a well of water springing up into everlasting life." John 4:14 (KJV)

As Daddy Gene and grandmother took me to church, it was the beginning of knowing the God who created me and this world along with the entire universe. Later accepting Him as my Lord and Savior and as a teacher in the physical sciences in the State of California it was very evident who my creator was and is.

I'm very thankful for the Sunday School teachers in Cripple Creek. By using the old flannel graph approach I never forgot the basic stories in the Bible.

Step-grandfather's Bible (small bible) fifty two years old.
Grandmother's Bible sixty two years old.

# The Deer Chase

What an exciting day for my cousin Buddy and I, as we were climbing the steep hill in front of grandmother's home in Cripple Creek. It was a beautiful day and there was radiance from God's creation from each and ever angle. We could see for miles with all trees in full bloom. There was water in the local reservoir below from all the Spring rains which helped to water the cattle, horses and other animals on Federal land. You could see the change of colors as they flowed through the morning hour and as haze met with your eyes in the distance so magnificent was its beauty to behold. What fragrance to ones nose and the awesome feeling would come over my cousin and I. A time to reflect on the beauty of God's creations and at the same time to just spend time with each other in the stillness of the day and absorb within our souls the real love before us which spoke no words, but yet a book within of endless stories.

Suddenly below us we spotted a young dear near the reservoir drinking water and observing the reflections before it. At first we didn't really know what to do as a pack of dogs from out of nowhere had been chasing the deer. We just made our assessments and thought to ourselves, what would happen if we bolted down the hill with a good speed and attempted to chase the deer on down the hill toward Cripple Creek? Well, that is just what we did and down the hill we went with full force being careful not to fall and roll down the hill and get hurt. The young deer first stood still and observed us as we continued to approach him. Without notice the deer bolted down the hill and headed straight for Cripple Creek. We continued our approach and soon reached the plain below near the old Mill Creek. The deer was becoming very excited and seemed to lose a sense of direction with buildings and other objects nearby. Finally he darted for the creek and went behind the old Crockett Store in the little village and leaped on to the road in town and ran down the street passing the old post office, gas station and noticed an opening leading beside an old home. The deer then leaped the small fence surrounding the front yard and headed toward the back yard of someone we didn't really know. To our amazement the dear ran through the backyard and started to leap another fenced area when suddenly the deer noticed the barking of ferocious dogs charged at the fence and the deer started to slip and slide and then bent his neck down and fell, apparently braking its neck.

An old man lived in the house and seeing what had happened, ran out of the house pulling from his pocket a big old Hawkbill knife and slitting the deer's throat, yelling at Buddy and I saying, "You boys better get out of here as I'm calling the Game Warden and you are going to jail." We didn't waste any time and ran home as fast as we could leaving no trail to follow and never telling anyone about our experience for the day that had been so serine and beautiful.

The old Cripple Creek Reservoir across from Francis
Mill Creek, behind Mrs. Henley's home
on the mountain where our deer chase
started.
Picture taken in the 1950's

# Catfishing in the Old Francis Mill Creek

It was a very hot and muggy day on August 11, 1967 in the little village of Cripple Creek, Virginia. It was always such a pleasure to visit with grandmother and Daddy Gene my step-grandfather, especially in the summer time some years later.

It was such a beautiful day even with the heat and being muggy, our son Tim King wanted to go fishing in the old Mill Creek flowing in front of grandmother's home. As a youngster, I too fished in the old Mill Creek many times when I was about the same age as our son Tim.

It was August 11, 1967 at about 8:55 in the morning when our son set out to drop his hook and line into the old Mill Creek. It was but just a few minutes when he felt a tug on his line and soon to his surprise he had caught a catfish weighing about a pound, and approximately eleven inches long. He was so excited and we just happened to have a camera… so now you too can see the picture of one very happy boy and we all were so proud of him as you see I too once stood in the same spot holding my catch too.

A wonderful and happy day!

A real catch of the day.
In the background, our daughter Lynn, son John and step-grandfather.

49

# Wayne's Catch

I tried, but you can't see my catch…

1948

# Colored Rocks in the Old Mill Creek

Out into the old Mill Creek my friend and I would go. His name being Nathaniel, but we all just called him "Nat" for short. He was my best friend and we shared so many wonderful times in the little village of Cripple Creek and old Mill Creek was our science laboratory and didn't even know it.

The most beautiful rocks covered the bottom of the old creek and so many of them were flat and easy to skip across the water as the creek wasn't too wide…maybe about six to eight feet when low, and very shallow in the summer months after most of the snow had melted.

Nat and I were about the same age, but he was one grade ahead of me in school. We attended the Cripple Creek School located about two miles from where we lived. The old school was built in 1895 and quite different from our schools today…anyway, let's get to the rocks.

At the time, Nat and I were about six or seven years old. We found so many beautiful and fascinating rocks. We didn't understand much about the rock cycle or have any idea what we were doing. All we understood about the rocks was, they were hard and some soft and made beautiful markings on each other. Later we discovered we had been experimenting with the now known "Streak Test" in geology in order to determined the chemical make up of different materials and composition. To us, it was just fun and filled our day with doing things with our hands and minds and learning something about the wonderful and beautiful earth God had made for everyone.

"What a wonderful day we had!"

One rock against another…the Streak Test.

The Streak Test

# Hog Killing Time

Hog killing time was quite an adventure in Cripple Creek; not really an adventure, but a time for the community to bring together those in the community preparing food and a few other supplies such as soap, for the hard days ahead.

Actually it was a real heartbreaking time seeing what was done for folks to survive the harsh winters from year to year. The hog killings were very necessary and many of the men in the community did participate in helping each other, which kept good communications with those living in the little village of Cripple Creek. The women also participated in the event and contributed much to this day.

As I remember, Mrs. Sophie Hale and her husband had the largest number of hogs in the community. To what extent they shared their hogs I'm not sure. Most of the folks had their property fenced off, helping to control other animals from roaming from one property to another. One thing for sure, hog meat was a very important part of everyone's diet and much care was taken in the preparation of the meat. It was just after World War II as I remember. People were still struggling for the essentials of life because of the United States Government issuing Food Rationing Stamps. This limited everyone during the six year war, killing an estimated 55 million people, both civilians and military. This was the worst war in human history.

As I remember, the hog killing took place along side the old Mill Creek, very near Crockett's General Store in Cripple Creek. For me to describe all the details about a hog killing, it would be very difficult. I do remember the hogs being brought to the pins along Mill's Creek in the months of January and February. The weather was an important factor due to possible spoilage and a loss of efforts in keeping the meat cold enough for storage in a smoke house. For the most part, people stored their pork for about a year and things had to be under control at all times.

Before the killing of the hogs, there had to be a time of preparation. Large containers (cast iron pots) had to be filled with water, and wood stored for the fires to be built hours prior to the killing. The water had to be scalding hot, and very sharp knives had been prepared for scraping off the hog's hair once placed into the hot boiling water. The sharp knives were used for sticking and bleeding the hogs, as well as the carving the carcass.

I do remember a .22 caliber rifle being used for the killing but know other methods were used as well. I really never enjoyed this period of time, but understood it was a necessary part of life in order to survive in times of shortages of food. At times folks would meet early in the morning in preparation for the slaughter. One thing I do remember was the smell coming from the area or hog pens and really didn't favor it all.

The hog was herded into a small area and soon one of the men prepared his rife for the kill. I still remember the poor hog making sounds of uneasiness looking to see what was going on. As the .22 rifle was ready for the kill, we were told to stay back from the hog and be still. Suddenly there was a " bang" and the animal fell to the ground quivering and it was time for someone to slit the throat of the hog in order for the blood to drain from an artery to preserve the meat. This was the time I considered to be sad yet knowing it was necessary for us to survive as a community.

After the bleeding process was over, it was time for the hog to be hoisted up and placed into the boiling hot water covering most of the body in order to scrape the hair from the animal. After a few minutes of soaking in the hot boiling water, it was time for scraping hair from the hog. Soon the sharp knives passed over the skin of the animal and the hair started falling into the water. After the hair was scraped off, it was time for the real task of gutting the old hog. The smell of the water and hog was one I didn't desire to be near…what a smell it was.

Before long the process of butchering started and much was to be done with almost every part of the animal. Usually a large table was set up and very sharp knives, saws and other necessary items were arranged for the arduous task of cutting the hog into quarters and removing the liver and other organs for processing. I personally don't remember all the details from this point but know a great deal of work was done for the proper use of the hog.

It wasn't until after World War II, much of the home hog killing stopped. People were more exposed to the local food stories for their supplies and times were improving.

For a more detailed story on hog killings in the early days of the nineteen hundreds, I suggest one read the following. The Foxfire Book and Foxfire 3, edited with an introduction by Eliot Wigginton. You will find many fascinating stories of the early days.

Another excellent story regarding hog killings is the Knotts Island Hog Killing by Tunis Corbell. His true story of the days when hogs were so very important in the early days as I have mentioned to you in my personal story.

Many of the young people today don't truly understand the harsh times many people endured in the early part of the last century in the United States and a large percentage of young people of today don't understand the real shortages of food and good water throughout the world as we know it today.

# Five Gallon Lard Cans Full of Silver Coins

Wow! Cans full of money…so many silver coins all over the place. My friend "Nat" and I were so very young at the time, about six or seven years of age and were invited to visit a friend of my grandmother's living next door to her. Her name was Mrs. Sophie Hale and there was always a strange odor in her house. She and her husband raised hogs and in order to get to her house, one would need to walk directly by the hog pens and boy did they stink…I can still smell the odor.

One thing for sure, once we made it past the stench of the hogs and so much mud (in winter), we entered Mrs. Sophie's front porch because of the unpainted structure, the elements had taken their toll on the old pine boards, and for a moment we thought we might fall through to the ground. Once we were inside of her home it was very dark and a strange feeling came over us. Clutter was from top to bottom. She collected everything it seemed. Pathways led from one place to another. Room by room we walked, praying along the way. We thought for a moment we might need a flashlight to find our way. We meandered from one place to another thinking we were entering some kind of ghost house and that it might be haunted as she was quite strange and not always friendly. For whatever reason she wanted us to see her treasure we'll never know, except we think it was to show us her wealth even with all the mess and the hogs. She made a good deal of money because when she opened the room where she stored her five gallon cans, they were filled with silver coins dating way back into the 1800's. "WOW," so many cans filled with more silver coins than we could have ever counted. She would just smile and was kind to us even with all the congestion.

Anyway, what a day with Mrs. Sophie Hale. As young boys and seeing so many coins we can't help but think, what ever happened to all the coins and to Mrs. Sophie and her husband?

Mrs. Sophie Hale's pig farm is in the distance with the tall barn. My grandparent's home with the white roof is across from the old car.

# The Old Greasy Pole
## (Dark Cave or Piper's Cave)

Down through the little village of Cripple Creek, Virginia we would go. My friend "Nat" and I, looking for another day of real adventure. We so enjoyed being together and looking for a real day of a great experience!

There was a very special cave (I think it's known as "Piper's or Dark Cave") not too far from my grandmother's home along a river where the American Indians lived years ago and we looked for Indian relics wherever we went. At times we had good finds. This old cave was filled with so many different and unique things. It was difficult to enter as a huge rock at the mouth of the cave was tilted and produced a small opening for us to squeeze through and thinking back, it was really dangerous. As I've read in past reports, the interior of the cave is much like Piper's Cave (?).

So here we go...after entering the cave we checked for snakes and bats using flashlights and praying the batteries would hold up for our journey. At times the bats would bolt by us and really shake our spirits. We thought it might be an evil spirit from one of the dead American Indians who once lived in the cave, but we didn't really believe this was possible because in Sunday School we were taught differently. We would walk close together, watching and feeling our way through the narrow passages leading toward what we called the old "Greasy Pole." This was nothing more than an old piece of petrified wood from so many, many years ago. The real scary thing was down below the old greasy pole was a fast flowing underground stream of water and if we slipped and went into the water we would be gone forever. Who knows where it might take us. We would be lost, gone, never to be found...buried alive underground. What a thought for such little ones as we. Once we made it beyond the old greasy pole and crossed the stream of water we would be safe enough to continue our journey.

Next, we spotted the stalactites, deposits of calcium carbonate, that are shapes of something like icicles hanging from the ceiling and water dripping from them to the cave floor creating stalagmites below forming an upside down stalactite. "WOW," what beautiful forms they were. Not too far from the newly discovered forms, Nat and I noticed the most unusual formation of all. It was the formation of what appeared to be a human leg, a woman's leg at that. We marveled at the precision, size, life likeness. How could this be? Only God could cause this to happen. We just made mental notes of what we observed and continued to look for more formations.

Later we discovered the opening to a huge room. It seemed to be so very different and as we had been told, the American Indians lived in this area many years ago. Only one thing stopped us from entering the room and that was because we had been told too, the room is filled with bones and other human remains, that could be very sacred and if we entered we might be in trouble. So, at this point we started out of the old cave, crossing the underground stream and up the old greasy pole of petrified wood. We were almost out when bats started flying overhead and frightening us. Soon we could see a beam of sunlight flowing through the opening, what a relief it was to be free and safe again.

What a day and experience it had been. Today it gives me chills to even think my friend and I entered such a place, but as young adventurous boys, we were protected by the hand of God. We never entered the old cave again.

As I remember in my drawing a long time ago.

# The Old Straw Tick Mattress Bed and the Chicken Feather Pillow

What an experience sleeping on the old straw tick mattress and feather pillows. Many Kings and Queens over the Centuries had their mattress made with straw and pillows stuffed with feathers.

At grandmother's home it was a special treat for me as a young boy to sleep on the old straw tick mattress and use the feather pillows. So many times as I crawled on to the bed, I could hear the popping of the straw beneath my knees. It sure made a strange sound and it took some time for me to get adjusted to the position I so desired in order for me to go to sleep, but I loved it anyway. As for the feather pillows, it too was something one would need time for adjustments. It was heavy, packed with so many feathers, and I always prayed the feathers were clean and didn't have anything on them. Guess I better not say too much more.

Many times while lying on the old straw tick mattress, I would listen to the flow of water in the old Mill Creek in front of grandmother's home. To me it was music to my ears. I would imagine being down by the creek bank with my fishing pole with line and hook catching the biggest catfish ever and filling up my string with the catches of the day. Of course I had to dream of the cornbread grandmother would fix, making my catfish dinner a real tasty meal. You see, grandmother used the old cast iron frying pan to fix the cornbread in her special oven, and when it was ready, it was golden brown and had an aroma to set off anyone's taste buds. With just the right amount of real butter applied from grandmother's churn to her cornbread, my whole world would change. "Wow!" I loved it.

So much for the night on the old straw tick mattress and feather pillow and now it's time to turn over and go to sleep and dream even more about the next day and what it'll hold for me.

# Refreshing "Spring Water" After Church

One of the most refreshing times I can ever remember on a Sunday afternoon was to bolt down to the old spring near the church in Cripple Creek. As I eluded to this memory in my short story previously, I must expand my thoughts. This spring was the most beautiful spring ever. Throughout the area of Cripple Creek and the old mines, many springs existed, but this one spring stood out so vehemently in my mind. With all the beauty surrounding it, one could just stand in awe looking at God's creations. The way the moss hung from the old willow tree and to listen as the wind blew through the trees and feeling the coolness of the day was so electrifying to me as a young boy. I just loved it! It was a time to be still and let God's creations teach and speak to me.

One particular memory was to watch the little minnows scurry about under water and tease me as they looked up at me. It was as though they understood what I was saying to them. At times they would swim up to my face, ever so close to the top of the water level. They had many different colors on them. Some were spotted and their fins were different too. So many species swimming around chasing after one another, daring the other to find them at times. I spent hours observing them, forgetting the time of day and would be late returning to grandmother's. What a wonderful day it was.

So many times we read in the Holy Scripture where Jesus referred to the running waters. The Living Water He offers to us as we listen and let His creations talk to us. His Spirit fills us to no end as we stand still and listen to Him.

Cripple Creek Church

Photos courtesy of Ruth Davidson

The old wagon bridge below the Cripple Creek Church.

65

Refreshing Bubbling Water

What a refreshing time for a cold drink of spring water bubbling up just for me.

# The Hawkbill Knife

I don't know if you know what a Hawkbill knife looks like, but it's a scary looking knife. The story I'm about to tell is a short one, but very true.

Many years ago, in the same little village of Cripple Creek, Virginia, a man named Jim Reeves (Betty Nucholls's father), lived just two doors down from my grandmother and Daddy Gene's home. Mr. Reeves was truly a mountain man and looked it too.

One day when I was walking down the little street leading to Cripple Creek's stores Mr. Reeves started walking toward me from his fenced yard and home. As a young boy of about six, I stared closely and intently at him and was afraid of him at first. He seemed to be nice, and polite but the closer I came toward him and the fence around his yard, he looked at me with very strange eyes, not blinking once and the closer we got to each other, I could see his unshaven beard and the old hat he was wearing pulled down over his eyes to some extent. Again, the closer we were, staring at one another I noticed his old overalls, and his right hand in his pocket. He was a short man and I wasn't sure what he was up to doing, and I wasn't sure what to say or do. I cautiously approached the yard toward him and as soon as I approach the fence, he suddenly pulled this strange and unusual knife from his pocket with a blade that looked like the bill of a hawk. He looked at me with a real growl and lunged forward toward me and said, "Come here boy, I'm going to cut your ears off." By this time my eye's were like saucers and ready to fall from my head. I immediately made a quick about turn and headed back toward grandmother's house running as fast as I could as my heart was pounding and racing ninety miles a second. There was no time lost as my little feet were pounding the asphalt road and I completely forgot where I was going.

After running so hard and desperately trying to find my way home, I rushed up the front door steps, bolting into the front room and immediately started explaining to grandmother what had happened, and that this man living down the street was coming after me and planning to cut off my ears and maybe feed them to his hogs. Grandmother and Daddy Gene thought this was so funny and broke into a delirious and uncontrollable laughter. Their faces were red from hearing my story and couldn't believe at first what I was telling them.  They continued laughing, explaining Mr. Reeves wouldn't hurt anyone intentionally and was just kidding with me. "Wow" was that a real relief.  I still had my ears and they didn't get fed to the hogs.

Remember, when you see a mountain man from Virginia, and he looks like Mr. Reeves, you better run until you know for sure he'll be your friend… as Mr. Reeves became my best friend in Cripple Creek.

What an experience for a little boy as I!

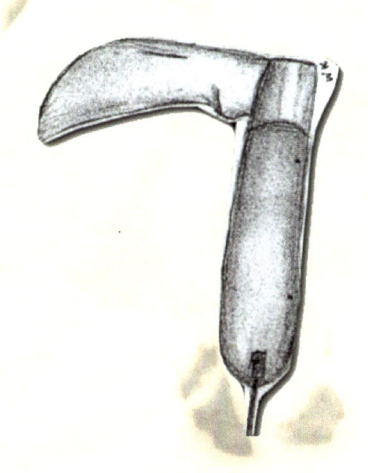

Hawkbill Knife

# Mrs. Davidson's Home in Cripple Creek, Virginia

What a wonderful home Mrs. Davidson owned. You'll see why I say her home was so wonderful and beautiful in the next part of my book dedicated to my friend "Nat." It was the uniqueness in design with all the ornate craftsmanship. The façade attracting anyone who might walk or drive by.

For many years her son "Nat" and I, who was my best friend, played for hours running around and playing games in her front yard. We so enjoyed running and being careful not to get stuck by one of the sword-shaped leaves protruding from the Yucca plants placed in strategic places.

My friend "Nat" had a very nice little woodshop in the backyard. The buildings were close together and Mrs. Davidson had a beautiful vegetable garden area near by too. We so enjoyed taking all the little pieces of wood in the woodshop and making different kinds of toys. At times the woodshop was a time out place for "Nat" when he didn't behave properly for his mother.

There were times when " Nat" would share all of his dad's military uniforms with me along with all the medals. Sure wish I could remember what the medals stood for…we were so young at the time and didn't understand the importance of each military medal.

One of the pieces of furniture inside Mrs. Davidson's home was the antique buffet. It was very fascinating with all the lions heads, and claw feet extending out onto the floor. The design was one from the Empire Period…1790-1830. The mirror was beveled and the buffet had four drawers with a lower section for storage. I purchased the buffet from Mrs. Davidson in the early 60's, picture on next page.

What wonderful memories I have of Mrs. Davidson's beautiful home and the yard my friend and I once played in.

Photo Courtesy Ruth Davidson

Mrs. Davidson's antique buffet located in her dining room adjacent to her kitchen.

March 20th, 1962

# Dedication

In fond memory of a dear childhood friend

Nathaniel Sidney Davidson

Captain United States Army

Vietnam

His last question to me prior to his death,

"Wayne, do you know Jesus as your Savior?"

# Dedication: Special Tribute to my friend Nathaniel Sidney Davidson, Captain U.S. Army

Nathaniel was a dear friend even though we were separated for many, many years. We played and roamed the hills of Cripple Creek for a number of years as young boys.

My mother and father were separated and divorced in 1943, which made it hard to have a place to call home. During World War II, I lived in many different places moving from one to another. After the war, I was able to stay and live with my grandmother in Cripple Creek from time to time and this is where I first met my dear friend Nathaniel called "Nat." So you see, we were very young at the time. I was born January 9, 1939 and "Nat" was born April 22, 1939.

Since "Nat" didn't have a father at home either, we found our lives woven together like a fabric as children and forever exploring the hills and caves of Cripple Creek whenever we had the chance or opportunity. At times we would lose track of time, getting in trouble with his mother or my grandmother because of arriving home too late. We tried to be on time, but you know what happens when kids get around water and find interesting things to do, you can't separate the kid from water, or as the old saying goes, "You can take the boy out of the country, but you can't take the country out of the boy." We enjoyed swimming in the stream of water called Cripple Creek, swinging from grapevines and falling into the water. It was a real treat eating wild grapes as well. What fun and pleasant days they were.

As I previously stated, we found a real interest in dissecting various crustacea from the old Francis Mill Creek and identifying rock materials as best as we could for our age at the time. Little did we know how these activities would one day relate to our lives in a very special way. We loved to explore, uncover, and relate our surrounds to everyday life.

Some of our discoveries such as the crayfish were very large and one thing for sure we didn't want to get pinched by their front walking legs. Generally we would remove the front walking legs first, just to be sure of no pain to us. These little creatures were active under rocks and would play games with us pulling themselves back into small areas beneath rocks and leaves, thinking we couldn't find them…but we did. It was exciting to dissect these unwilling ones, but we discovered how many of their systems worked over time. One thing for sure, they are very fast as they propelled themselves backwards.

Other little animals we discovered were the Central Stoneroller and Bluehead Chub minnows and many other species. These little ones played games with us as well. We would find large rocks in the creek with crevices and if there wasn't enough water in the crevice openings, we would fill the openings with more water. Something like a tide pool found along a coastal area when the tides are low. We would locate different little minnows such as the Central Stoneroller and Bluehead Chub and use small nets to catch them in and place them in the pool of water on the rocks. Then we would count the number of our catch and talk about their colors and how they would swim from one point to another. The Central Stoneroller would feed from the bottom of the stream, eating small plants, animal matter and green algae from rocks. The little Bluehead Chubs enjoyed building castles in the streams with small pebbles known as nests for their fertilized eggs in a dome-like shape and dared anyone to touch their accomplishments. We had to be careful at times because if it was very hot on a summer day, the temperature of the rock would increase and make it difficult for the little creatures to live. Many were very small, several inches long and they seemed to always like to play games like the crayfish…trying to escape from our capture. We just had fun and learned things too, much of which happened later in life.

Since the area of Cripple Creek was so very unique, "Nat" and I would also find many different colored rocks in Mill Creek and many times the rocks were different colors and soft. We soon learned by striking one rock against another it would leave a color on a flat rock. Then we would find another different colored rock and do the same thing…one rock against another and finally we would have all different colors on one good size flat rock. Not knowing once again that we had just discovered a system known as the streak test to geologists. Not too bad for us as kids just playing in a creek.

Now you have some idea as to why we were always getting in trouble with those in charge. Many times they didn't understand the importance it was for us to discover our little world. As you've read in some of the other stories, "Nat" and I found pleasure in doing so many things together, and this even meant spending time together even when we were in trouble. When it was time to face correction for being late getting home, we would share our time together in the woodshop set aside by "Nat's" mother. The room was filled with small pieces of wood and lots of nails. We had to create all kinds of things and not waste our time doing nothing. So we designed all kinds of little wood vehicles and the like…buildings and more buildings. We made airplanes, cars, trucks, and tried to make things move in different directions…we just had fun while being taught corrections and not to be late from our explorations.

This kind of bonding as young children can't be bought with money. It's irreplaceable and a commodity if I may say so. We learned so much playing together and sharing our thoughts and love for each other.

Too many children today are facing major problems with the culture they live in. The experience of natural surroundings are foreign to many. More and more communities of young and old are forced into major cities. There is less and less continuity at the old supper table sharing their day's activities. People are living too fast. As one little boy about six years old named Miguel, responded to a missionary lady who was trying to explain God's love in the streets of a major city. She explained to little Miguel God's love is like the beautiful mountains with streams of fresh clear water flowing over the rocks making you feel good inside and refreshed. He responded, "Hey lady, is God's love anything like the stream of water that flows down the dirty gutter? You see, I've never been outside the big city before." Too many times we make assumptions before we speak.

I'm very pleased with all the natural experiences "Nat" and I had together as young children and no amount of money could ever replace our friendship. I'm sure many other children in Cripple Creek could share their lives in much the same manner as I have and even better.

I'm also most grateful to know my friend "Nat" accepted Christ as His personal Savior, and that God allowed our paths to cross once again before his untimely death. I thank God that He led our footsteps as young children to know Him.

It's the fruit of the Spirit that brings meaning to all life. "...love, Joy, peace, longsuffering, gentleness, goodness, faith, meekness, temperance: against such there is no law." Galatians 5:22-23 (KJV)

The nine fruits can be broken into three groups. Group one: Love, joy and peace. We should display in our lives the love of God to others with joy in our hearts and peace with calmness in all we do. Group two: Longsuffering, gentleness and goodness. May we approach others with longsuffering coupled with gentleness and show goodness toward each other. Group three: Faith, meekness and temperance. May our faith be reflected in God and believing He will sustain us as we walk through life, being meek in all we do with humility and temperance. May our walk be under control, in moderation with self-restraint.

Finally, let us remember that the nine fruits of the Spirit are like a fabric, woven together with all threads working as a whole, strengthening each other, keeping unity at the same time and being a functional body as our lives should be in integrity and character.

"Now abideth faith, hope, charity, these three; but the greatest of these is charity." 1 Corinthians 13:13

Nathaniel Sidney Davidson
Fort Jackson South Carolina
1961

Nathaniel S. Davidson
Full Dress Uniform
Commissioned Officer
Captain U.S. Army

Nathaniel S. Davidson
Captain U.S. Army
Vietnam 1969

Captain Nathaniel S. Davidson congratulating U.S. Army personnel for their military accomplishments.

Fort George G. Meade, Maryland
1969

# U.S. Army and Foreign Awards

Nathaniel S. Davidson
Captain, U.S. Army

Bronze Star Medal

Army Commendation Medal

Army Good Conduct Medal

Vietnam Service Medal

National Defense Medal

The Republic of Vietnam Campaign Medal

Meritorious Unit Citation

Republic of Vietnam Gallantry Cross w/Palm Unit Citation Badge

82

Expert Badge w/Rifle Bar

    Please accept my deepest apology if I have overlooked an award, citation or any other recognition made for my friend Nathaniel S. Davidson for his dedicated and honorable service to preserve our freedoms in the United States of America as he served as an Army Captain with honor, dignity, pride, integrity, gallantry and perseverance.

## THE PRESIDENT OF THE UNITED STATES OF AMERICA

*To all who shall see these presents, greeting:*

*Know Ye, that reposing special trust and confidence in the patriotism, valor, fidelity and abilities of* NATHANIEL SIDNEY DAVIDSON *, I do appoint* him a reserve Commissioned Officer *in the*

## Army of the United States

*to date as such from the* sixteenth *day of* November *, nineteen hundred and* sixty-six *. This Officer will therefore carefully and diligently discharge the duties of the office to which appointed by doing and performing all manner of things thereunto belonging.*

*And I do strictly charge and require those Officers and other personnel of lesser rank to render such obedience as is due an officer of this grade and position. And this Officer is to observe and follow such orders and directions, from time to time, as may be given by me, or the future President of the United States of America, or other Superior Officers, acting in accordance with the laws of the United States of America.*

*This commission is to continue in force during the pleasure of the President of the United States of America, for the time being, under the provisions of those Public Laws relating to Officers of the* **Armed Forces of the United States of America** *and the component thereof in which this appointment is made.*

*Done at the City of Washington, this* sixteenth *day of* November *in the year of our Lord one thousand nine hundred and* sixty-six *, and of the Independence of the United States of America the one hundred and* ninety-one *.*

*By the President:*

Kenneth G. Wickham
Major General
The Adjutant General.

Stanley R. Resor
Secretary of the Army

DD FORM 1A
1 AUG 60

*The United States of America*

*honors the memory of*

*Nathaniel S. Davidson*

*This certificate is awarded by a grateful nation in recognition of devoted and selfless consecration to the service of our country in the Armed Forces of the United States.*

*President of the United States*

# Ruth Davidson

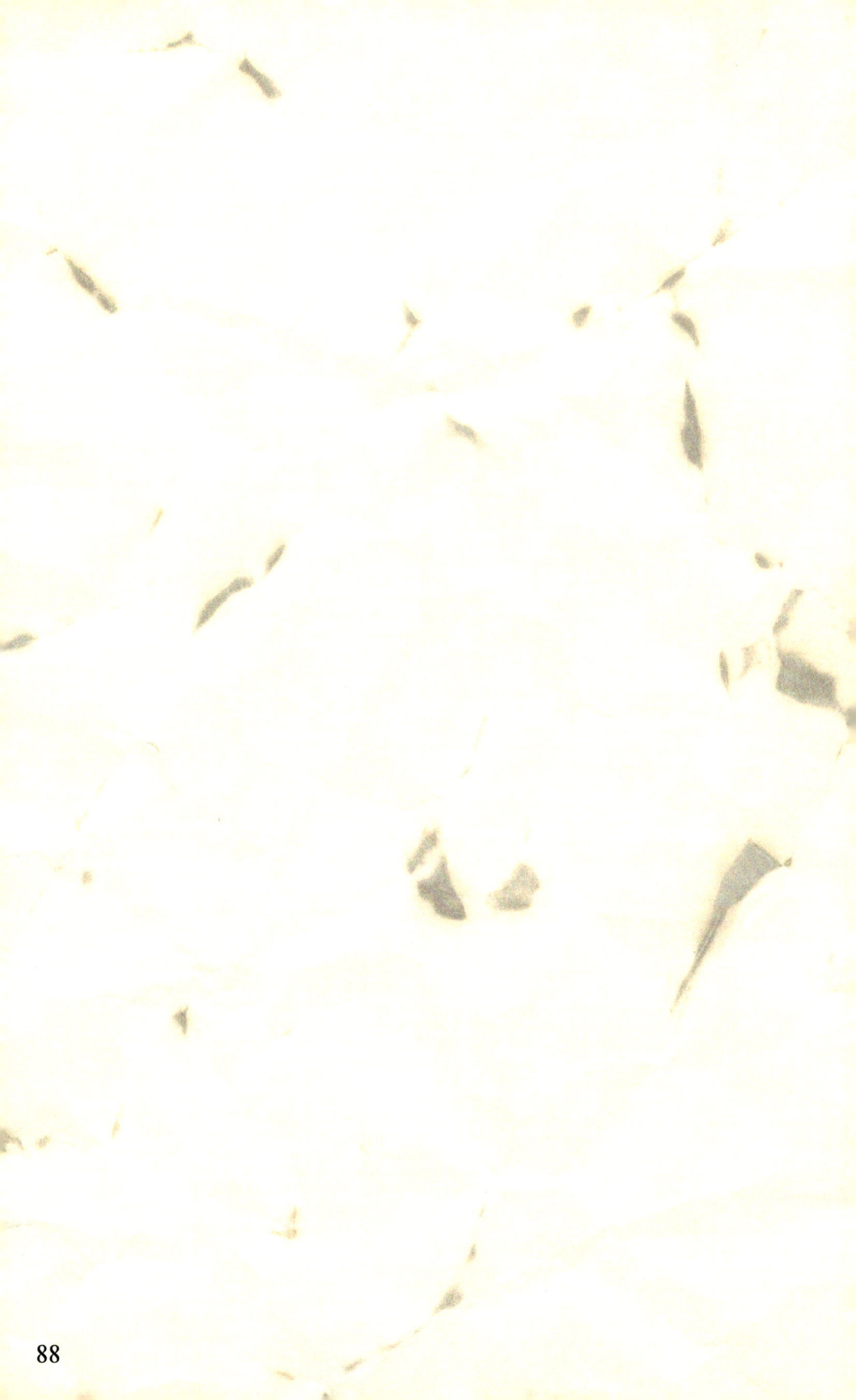

## Ruth Davidson

In deep appreciation to Ruth Davidson for all her devotion and care for her late husband Nathaniel "Nat" Davidson.

Without question her love, commitment and devotion gave "Nat" a sense of comfort, love, peace and companionship.

"Nat" May 3, 1948

"Nat" 1947

Mrs. Macia Davidson 1945
"Nat's" mother

"Nat" 1956

90

"Nat's" home, date unknown

1962

Hattie May King
(Wife)

Francis Mill Creek

Original creek locations
where "Nat" and I discovered
many crayfish and minnows.

Mrs. Henley's home in the background.

92

The old wagon bridge and swimming hole.
Photo postcard courtesy of Ruth Davidson

1946
Eva Gentry
Ernest Worrell
Cripple Creek

Photos courtesy of Mrs. Pearl C. Woods

1941
George Wright
Johnny Jones
Cripple Creek

Cripple Creek School constructed in 1895 and abandoned in 1952.
Grades 1-7

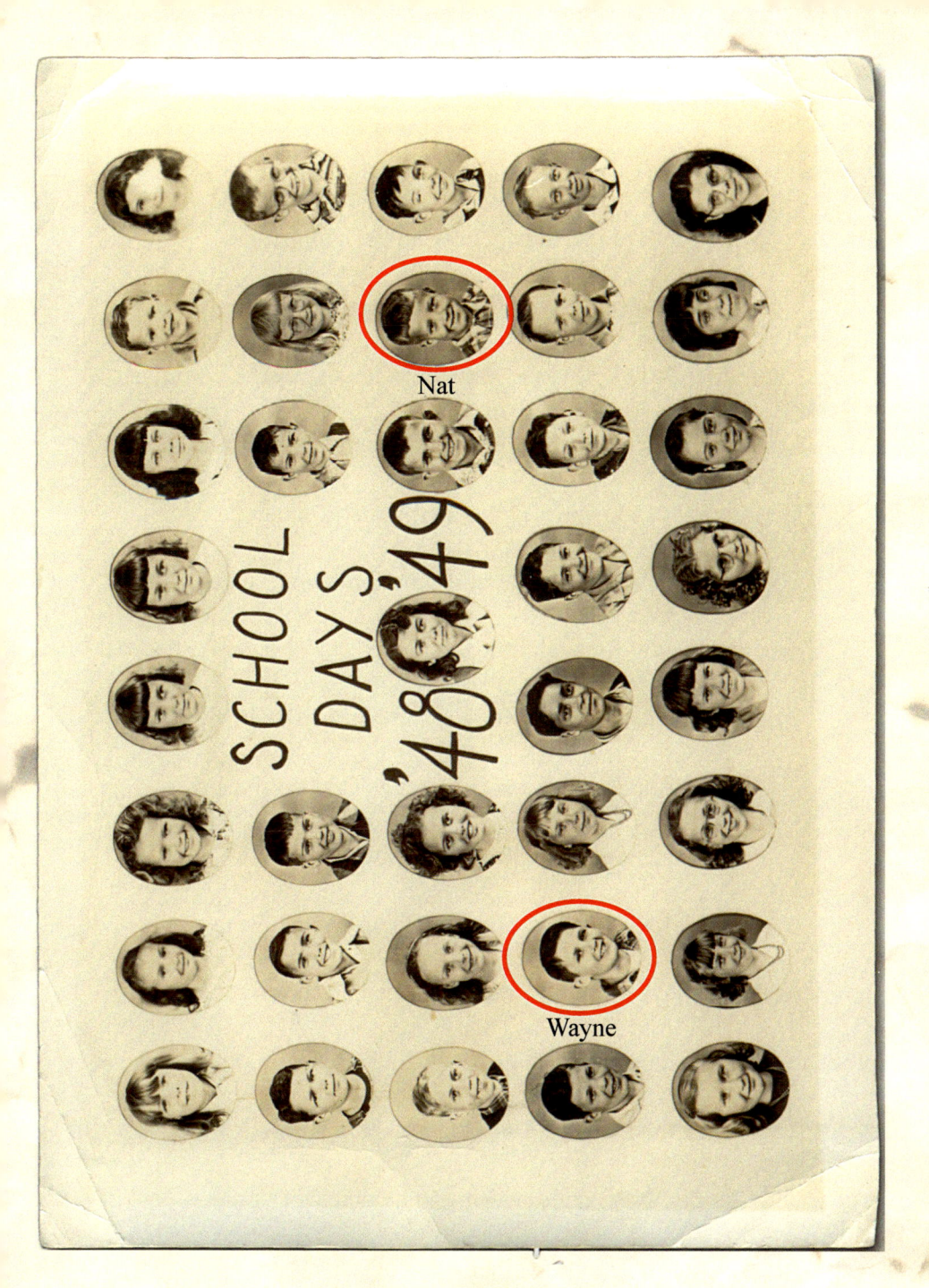

School Days 1948-1949
Miss Peggy Allison Teacher

Nathaniel S. Davidson third row second student on left.

Morris W. King forth row second student on right.

95

# Friends

Who are true friends?

True friends believe in each other.

True friends will always trust in each other.

True friends will always share their hurts and shortcomings.

True friends in Christ will confide in each other with confidence, and love.

True friends are loyal to each other, with no slander, or malice.

True friends live to encourage and build each other up.

True friends pray for each other each day and give praise to God.

True friends listen to each other, and listen to their soul's cry.

True friends forgive and forget as God forgives us.

True friends will pick you up when you fall down.

True friends give hugs and tell you Jesus loves you.

True friends are always there for you even when all the silver and gold is gone.

True friends turn hate into love as Jesus did and we too must do the same.

True friends will seek the true Spirit of God and help you to listen to His still voice

True friends are humble, gentle, willing to be there for you in a time of need.

True friends will feel your loneliness, catch your tears as they fall and love you.

True friends will always tell you Jesus loves you and will be with you.

True friends will lay down their lives for you. "Greater love hath no man than this, that a man lay down his life for his friends." John 15:13

# Artifacts in the Garden

I have always been fascinated by the American Indian and believe there is some American Indian blood flowing in my veins. If there is any truth in the findings by my cousin Carlene Sandhagen , and I pray there is, my great-grandmother would be that of Sara Lawhorn. Maybe someday we'll know the real truth, but until that day, I'll just keep looking for American Indian relics.

Mrs. Davidson's garden was directly behind her beautiful home as described previously. She gave me permission to look for American Indian Relics in her garden one day and I jumped at the challenge. For me to find a relic was always the highlight of the day. I so enjoyed running out to any newly cultivated ground on a small knoll near a creek as I had read in books that most points or arrowheads and tools were made in areas like these. Since the old Mill Creek was so close, Mrs. Davidson's home would be ideal for such a find of artifacts.

On this day it would be a very exciting one! I hadn't been in Mrs. Davidson's garden for very long where I found evidence of flint and chert, and low and behold there before my very eyes lay a beautiful bird tip as we call them. A very small point used by the American Indian for killing small fowl. I continued my search and found a number of points (see picture next page). Knowing what I know now about American Indian Artifacts I should have continued my search in depth.

Another area for artifacts was discovered by my friend "Nat" close to my grandmother's home near a bridge being constructed by contractors. The new bridge was a part of the main road through Cripple Creek and while dirt was being moved, "Nat" found a beautiful spear point made of flint or quartz. Beings "Nat" was so young, Mr. Jim Reeves, living a few doors down from my grandmother, talked "Nat" out of the spear point.

What stories "Nat" and I shared recently before his untimely death in April 2007.  Even though we were about three thousand miles apart, " Nat" said to me as his friend, "Wayne, if I still had the spear point, I would send it to you."   I was so surprised to have him say this to me as I didn't know the story about the find until recently.  I assumed he said what he did because of our friendship.   What a long lost friendship of sixty years that was reunited for a few more months of life on this earth.

"Nat" will always remain a friend in my heart forever.

Native American Indian Artifacts discovered in and around Cripple Creek, Virginia

1948-1949

# A Day of Antiquing with my Dad, Dillard King

It all started many years ago while my wife and children were on vacation in nineteen sixty- two with my dad in Greensboro, North Carolina. We were visiting him while on military leave from California, and it was suggested we go antiquing with a small trailer and our limit of funds would be a total of twenty- five dollars ($25.00) for the whole day. Twenty-five dollars ($25.00) was a fair amount of money in those days, anyway for us it was.

We packed up things, hooked up the trailer, filled the car with gas and set out for Cripple Creek, Virginia some one hundred and twenty miles away. We really didn't know just how the day would turn out, but praying it would be a very successful time and for us to enjoy the family being together with my dad, my wife and our two children at the time…in time there would be one more son, named John.

Lover's Leap, Bobby Porter, Barbara Porter, Hattie King
Picture January 1993

As we proceeded on our way northwest from Greensboro, North Carolina, there seemed to be a special time of love and sharing as we drove over and through the hills of the Carolina's, and soon passed through an area west of Stuart, Virginia, known as Lover's Leap. The meandering through the hills didn't seem to bother anyone, and the stop at Lover's leap was very special as one could see for miles and miles from the old rock wall constructed many years ago. So it goes, Lover's Leap was known for two young lovers falling to their death nearby and hence, "Lover's Leap."

One of the things that made this day very special was being with my dad. I didn't get to be with him very much as a child growing up as mother and father were separated when I was only three years old. Now that I was grown, in the military service, married and we had two children, it helped in many special ways.

As we were meandering through the mountains of Virginia with our little trailer, and passing through Hillsville, Virginia, where the famous glass bottle house, The House of a Thousand Headaches, is located, we were so happy and excited to be looking for good deals on antiques. The scenes were simply breath taking and we all looked with awe as we drew closer to the Appalachian Mountains near Cripple Creek, Virginia.

THE BOTTLE HOUSE, HILLSVILLE, VA.

THE HOUSE OF A THOUSAND HEADACHES

## THE HOUSE OF A THOUSAND HEADACHES

As we continued our journey, we soon approached the City of Wytheville, Virginia. We surely knew we would be only approximately ten to fifteen miles from Cripple Creek and looking forward to a good find of antiques.

After arriving in Cripple Creek, one of our first stops was to visit with Mrs. Davidson (my friend Nat's mother, previously mentioned) as she once mentioned she would sell her old Empire designed buffet (1790-1830) to me. As we all considered the offer to her, we settled for a reasonable amount of good old American currency. We then loaded the monstrosity in our trailer. This buffet was huge as you see from the picture . The main problem was to get this monster home without breaking anything, especially the mirror. We thanked Mrs. Davidson for the opportunity to have such as find. She was very happy as we were too.

Mrs. Davidson's antique buffet located in her dining room adjacent to her kitchen. Not the original room as seen in the above picture…March 20th 1962

    From this point we continued down the street to the old Crockett General Store where I remembered as a boy, the old ring box telephone hanging just inside the door to the right as one walked into the store.  The old telephone was gone and a newer model took the place of the once very reliable ring box which hung there for so many, many years.  I questioned Mr. Crockett as to what happened to the old telephone?  Well he said, "It's back here some place under all these pop bottles."   As he proceeded to locate the old telephone, he kept saying, "I don't know if I should sell this ring box or not, but guess it won't hurt anything as it's of no use to us since we have this modern one on the wall."   The modern telephone he referred to was a small oak box telephone with two bells on top, a ringer, mouthpiece, and receiver.  After a short time Mr. Crockett sold us the telephone for fifteen dollars.  Everyone was happy and we were on our way to another home a few miles away where I once got my haircut.

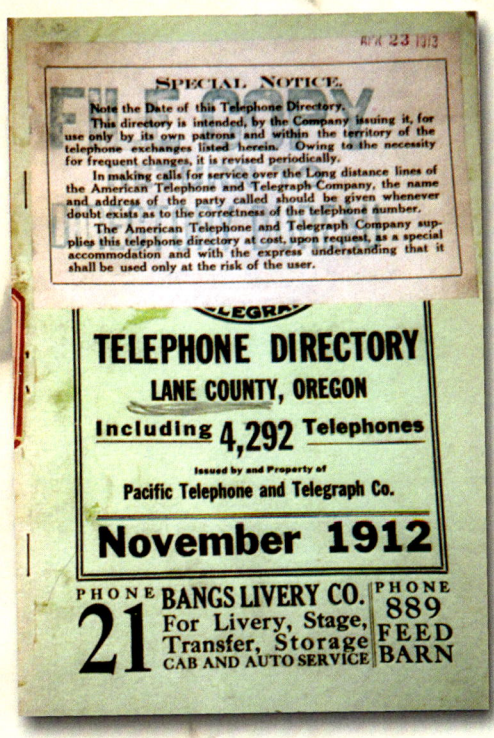

The old ring box telephone so popular for so many years that helped change the world we live in today. Wish I had an old telephone book from Virginia, but here's a picture of what they once looked like.

103

Pop bottles and telephones, Crockett's Grocery Store Cripple Creek, Virginia. My wife might kill me if I sell this phone to you.

It was very, very interesting as we approached the little home and knocked on the door, seeking other telephones and parts. From what I remember, the gentleman living there said to me, "I remember you, you're the little King boy that once lived with your grandmother and I cut your hair occasionally." I replied yes, and that was many, many years ago. We all had a good laugh and continued our conversation about what we were up to…looking for antiques, especially old telephones. It just happened he had a few parts, but no complete telephones. We completed our stay and from what I remember he gave us the parts he had. We were so appreciative, thanking him and went on our way.

Picture of one of the old houses near Cripple Creek, similar to one I once visited for a haircut.

Photo courtesy of Ruth Davidson

After leaving the home where I once received my haircuts as a young boy, we headed back to Cripple Creek. It just so happened I inherited the old hair clippers from my dad used by my grandfather James Henry King for cutting the hair of my dad, Morris Dillard King, my uncles, Keister King, Jimmy King and Billy King. Please see family picture. The same type clippers were used for cutting my hair. "BOY," they could really pull your hair and bring crocodile tears if the clippers were dull.

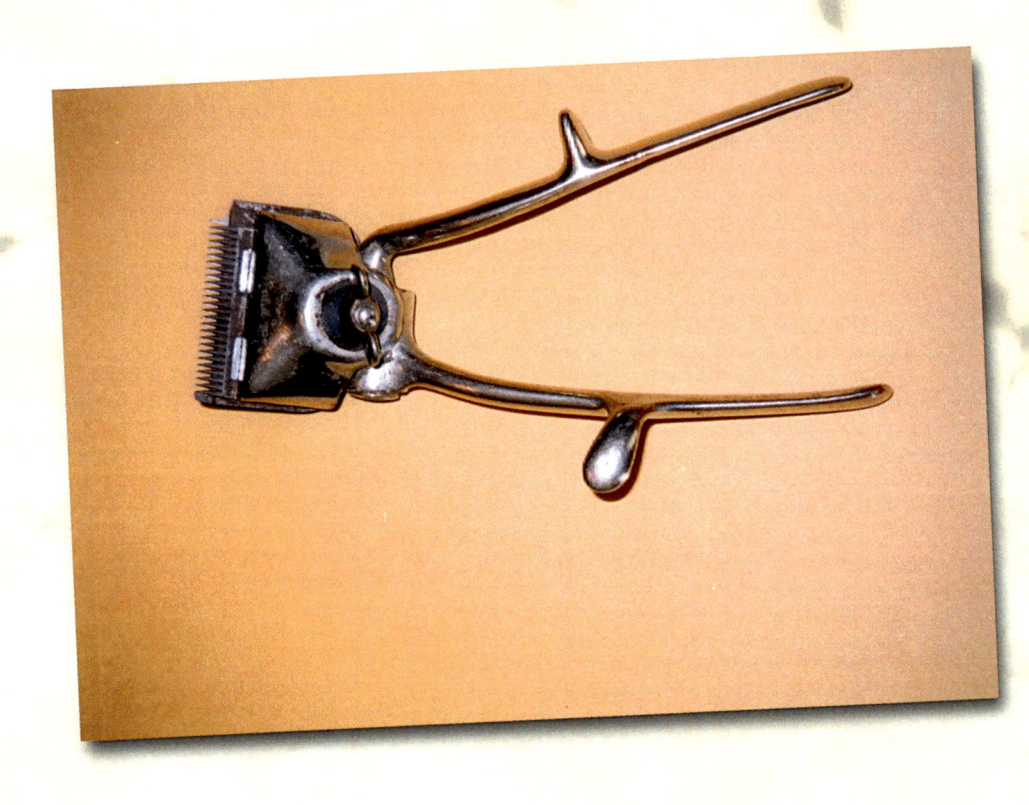

James Henry King's antique hair clippers.

Back row, left to right, Jimmy, Keister, Dillard, (my father) and Billy King
Front left Aunt Doris and Aunt Edna Earle.

    After a wonderful day, we headed home for Greensboro, but on the way we still had a few dollars to spend. We stopped at a small antique shop and I spotted a beautiful coffee grinder located on a mantel over the fireplace. It looked authentic, smelled authentic and even felt authentic. The owner explained "I can't sell the coffee grinder to you as my wife would kill me." My dad didn't say anything at the time and the gentleman thought for a few more minutes and said "I guess I can sell the coffee grinder to you and pray I live through the night." Needless to say I was very happy at the time, so I purchased the coffee grinder and we were on our way home.

    Since my wife and I didn't have a way to transport our finds back to California, we stored our antiques with my dad until we could have them shipped out west. After returning home in California, I contacted my dad and requested the items be shipped to us. Well, dad said, "It may be a problem as I discovered the coffee grinder was a replica and I sold it for a few dollars over what you paid for it."

We can all learn a lesson when going antiquing and not knowing what to look for. It sure taught us a lesson and never again did we go antiquing. My dad shipped the buffet to us, but wanted the old telephone from Crockett's General Store. I don't know what he did with it at the time, but wish now I still had the original. As for the buffet, it was stored and moisture caused a major problem with it, and it also was dropped. Finally, the buffet was sold to another antique deal in Hanford, California, repaired and placed on Tagus Ranch in Tulare, California. But guess what? I still have the key to the old buffet.

What a wonderful day antiquing!

The old coffee grinder with a few pounds of coffee directly from Central America we purchased years ago…frozen in bags.

Some of my dad's (Dillard King) antique telephones and clocks. Most of his collection was located in his shop. He loved collecting telephones, clocks and coffee grinders. He was known throughout Virginia and North Carolina as the clock man. He could fix anything.

Dad's clock shop.

# The Old Schoolhouse in Cripple Creek, Virginia

Miss Peggy Allison
1948-1949

As you can see from the artist rendering and photo of the old elementary school house in Cripple Creek, Virginia, it was a small building with few students.

Miss Allison was my third grade teacher and I might say a wonderful and inspiring one at that. She never raised her voice to the students and had excellent control in the classroom. One thing for sure, if you were in trouble and got a spanking at school, you surely would receive a reminder of the same when you arrived home. There wasn't any room for any errors. The psychology stick or paddle was always near to remind one of who was in charge…not the student for sure.

Another good reason for order and control in Miss Allison's classroom was the number of grade levels in her class. She would assign the first row of seats to grade one, second row, grade two and the third row grade three. There was a total of approximate thirty- six students. This wasn't always true, but varied from time to time.

The extra assignment given me in the winter months, was to secure coal from outside the classroom. I sure didn't like to get the black mess on my hand's as it was difficult to wash off. But one thing for sure, coal would give off a good deal of heat and a lot of black smoke. I enjoyed watching the coal burn. When I opened the door for stoking, it would glow a very bright orange and yellow color when oxygen rushed into the chamber. The old potbelly stove in the classroom had to be kept filled with coal in order to maintain a constant room temperature as the floor and walls weren't insulated many years ago.

I certainly feel a good basic learning of the three "R's" came from Miss Allison. She was always willing to help a student and assist in any way possible to see you succeed. There was time for students to learn and not be so rushed. She expected all of us to put forth our best in whatever we were doing and not goof off in class. The classroom was one of respect and not a place to cause troubles.

Another fascinating part of the old classroom was the inkwells. We were required to practice our manuscript writing each day. I always thought it fun to dip into the inkwell and practice writing and to do a little drawing from time to time. Of course this was after completing our assigned task of writing…never to goof off…Ha! Ha!

Guess I better bring this little story to an end. The memories of yesterday still permeate my mind and bring back the basics of life and what it has taken to journey this far. If it wasn't for the help of our Father in heaven, I just wouldn't be here today.

Cripple Creek School constructed in 1895 and abandon in 1954.
Grades 1-7.

Additional room some years later for more classroom.
Drawing Courtesy of Phyllis M. Umberger

# Time for Recess

(Miss Peggy Allison)

What a fun time at recess in the old Cripple Creek School. As I've stated in my previous story about the classroom and how Miss Allison conducted her classes, it's time for a little fun at recess.

In the late summer, autumn, winter and spring, days were filled with so much fun. I can never remember a time when students would get into fights or cause major problems. As late summer fell upon us and the leaves on the trees were preparing to change their colors, it was a time of feeling so free.

Outside games we played were very limited. Since World War II was over and more items such as rubber, steel, tin and paper products were more plentiful, we had baseballs, footballs and the like. We would play baseball and football (tag), but usually we didn't have teams as organized as we do today. We played simple games, Red Rover, Red Rover, tag, seek and find, and other simple games. When winter arrived, we had snow on the near by hills in front of the school across the main highway leading to Wytheville and we didn't need road guards as we do today. Students respected the traffic, used common sense, using their heads when crossing the roadway. It was wonderful to climb the hills and slide down on our new sleds made of wood, and metal…and we didn't need yard duty teachers (with respect) yelling at us. Times have sure changed…"WOW!"

Some of the inside games were playing checkers, having a spelling bee or not a game, but just visiting each other during recess in friendly talk. We talked about our home life and what was going on regarding our chores in helping our parents or grandparents. Maybe how to make wood toys, look for American Indian artifacts near by. Students shared points of interest to help each other.

Yes, it was fun in Miss Allison's class at recess and at lunchtime as well, which was about an hour. We all had packed lunches and much of which hasn't changed too much over the years, except now one must be careful with the peanut butter and jelly sandwiches. Fruits and vegetables are about the same, except they are so contaminated with chemicals one never knows what may happen.

Times change and so it goes…another story will be written someday and nothing will be the same.

Hill in front of Cripple Creek School.
A fun place to play.

# Quiet Time "Lights Out"

One thing for sure, when living with my grandparents in Cripple Creek and it was 8:00 o'clock P.M., it was time for "Lights Out." The amazing thing was, we all slept in the front room during the winter months. My grandmother and step-grandfather, daddy Gene, slept in a double wide bed and I had a small cot along a wall and corner. This helped to conserve energy as we had the old potbelly stove in the front room as I've spoken of previously in another story. One thing I really didn't enjoy was getting up after hours and having to use the old slop jar in the cold closet on the back porch and then the next day, cleaning out the stinking thing. It was everyone's use during the night unless of course they wanted to head for the outhouse some fifty feet outback. I was in the third grade at the time and living with my grandparents, so there were no questions asked when it was quiet time.

My step-grandfather, (Daddy Gene) owned an old Philco radio as best I remember. Its design was like a steeple or church. It was light tan and varnished. The radio was made of oak wood and was beautiful. The dial was round inside with a window open showing different radio stations by numbers. The face structure had a small dial to select the proper channel. We didn't have too many radio stations in those days.

Daddy Gene didn't want anyone to ask question about anything and to remain very, very quiet as it was hard to hear what was being said on the news channel. Sometimes the static was so loud it almost hurt one's ears.

After a thirty minute period of time it was "Lights Out" and go to sleep. I really have to say, it was a special time as there were nights when a story would be on and no news. One could always imagine what might happen next in a good short story of some kind.

A time to never forget.

A very quiet street and a very quiet time for rest at grandmother's.

# "Lights Out"

What changes have occurred in my life time. There were times of no electricity in many homes in America and all we had for light in the evening time was the old oil lamp. We lowered the wick by hand and made sure the flame was out before going to bed.

The old lamp still works when the power goes off.

# Grandmother's Old Churn-Homemade Butter

Grandmother's old churn (made of stoneware) was always ready to go for a handy hand…up and down and no questions asked. One thing for sure, it took a good deal of time and energy when making good old homemade butter.

It was an exciting time after the cow(s) were milked and grandmother prepared the milk by placing it in a dry and cool place. She always had a special way of preparing things and I may not remember all the details, but here goes. First, I could hear grandmother singing and smiling as she scurried from one place to another. She was so happy. As soon as the milk was cooled and ready for the cream to be skimmed off the top, she would use a cream- skimmer when she had the opportunity as she didn't always have proper utensils for the job and would many times find other ingenious ways to remove the cream without causing problems. The objective was to recover the cream from the milk and allow the milk to fall back into its proper container, thereby, removing the cream for churning in her beautiful ceramic churn.

Now comes the churning of the cream. The object was to place the cream in a churn, putting on the top of the churn a churn lid with a hole in the center of the lid for the dasher, known as a stick with a round wooden board attached to it for beating the cream, thereby making the butter. The up and down movement helped to produce the yellow fat from the buttermilk, leaving the good old homemade butter. As tradition has it, a song or two may be heard from the one doing the churning just to pass the time away…such as…

Butter, butter don't be so lazy. Let's make some butter out of this fresh sweet cream…such a pleasant dream…please come butter, please come butter…

By: Hattie King

I always loved the buttermilk. When grandmother prepared her best of cornbread made in an old cast iron skillet, I would get me a big glass and place the buttermilk in it, then put it into the old icebox until chilled. Later I would take the fresh delicious cornbread and mix the buttermilk and cornbread together, eating it with a spoon…"WOW!" How scrumptious to the senses. I loved it.

Well, for the final word about the making of the butter, grandmother would place her beautiful butter molds or dishes, (cut crystal glass with beautiful designs) out and place the yellow butter into each of them. What a smile and proud look appeared on her face as she looked at the final craftsmanship in making homemade butter! she'd sit down and would say, "It's done and over with, praise God!"

Ceramic churns used for making butter.

Picture courtesy of Dairy Antiques
Paul and Linda

An old fashioned crystal glass butter dish, similar to what grandmother once used for her butter. Sorry I don't have an original from grandmother's kitchen but my wife's (Hattie King) will surely do.

# Crockett's General Store and The Old Telephone

With no doubt, as I've previously described in my story about Exciting Bus Ride and Lunch with Grandmother, the times I spent in Crockett's Old General Store was a blessed one I'll never forget.

It was always a joy to hear Mr. Crockett, owner of the old store say, "Good morning young man, you're the King boy that lives down the street with your grandmother aren't you? And you have your friend with you, Nat, Mrs. Davidson's son…what a great team you two make always exploring in the creek below and looking for the unusual things when I see you." Then he would just laugh and say, "What can I help you with today?" Nat and I would give him a big smile and look directly at his old, but big candy case, something similar to Mr. Kirby's down the street, a smaller store, from Mr. Crockett's General Store. After a few moments of eye contact and our mouths drooling with anticipation for a piece of the colorful strips of candy, Mr. Crockett would smile with love and a twinkle in his eye and say, "Well guys, you've convinced me for a sample, (As Mr. Crockett knew we had little money in those days with World War II still raging.) here you go." We would smile, thank him and out the door we would go and head for the creek looking for more exciting adventures for the day. Our days were not always planned, as one adventure may turn into a dozen or more…we just loved to be adventurous and encouraged each other along the way, and with support for each other, we had more and more fun learning about God's creation.

To add just a little more flavor to the story, I'll describe a little more about the inside part of the wonderful old store. One of the first things one would see when entering the store, was to the right of the front door, the old oak ring box telephone . To my heart it was a treasure and one that made me think about what makes this thing work. As a little guy of about six years of age at the time, I always wanted to talk into the transmitter and hear the operator say, "Information Please."  So many times I would hear people say, "More gossip goes on over them wires than anyone can believe." It seemed the operator knew everything first- hand as she didn't need to read the newspaper about everybody, and she was always a help when one was in need. Below is an example of one conversation of many years ago when the operator would say "Information Please."

122

# Information Please

My name is Wayne and how many times do I remember picking up the old telephone receiver from the oak ring box telephone and hearing the operator say, "Information Please." I wasn't too sure about how to use this invention as I spoke into the mouthpiece or transmitter—this black round thing filled with little holes in the middle of it, which looked like a horn. At times I could hear an echo as I held the receiver.

I was such a young boy of about six years old at the time and didn't fully understand how all these things worked, but I did know there seemed to be another person on the other end of the line somewhere in this box and if you said anything, this person would say "Information Please" and answer any question you may ask. She was very smart.

This little story is about what happened to a little boy, namely me, on one sad day that did turn bright when I couldn't find my grandparents in Cripple Creek. You know what can happen when you're young, scared and there's no one to help you…especially when you're about six years old. The "Information Please" sure helped me on this one day long ago giving me help even when Dr. Grubb (our local doctor) was out visiting a patient. Many times he would ride his horse to find and help the sick.

Well, here's my story. I was really feeling sad one lonely afternoon after returning from Cripple Creek School. I walked into my grandparent's home and found no one. You see this was a time at the close of World War II and things weren't the same. I didn't know where my mother was and dad left home when I was only three. This is the reason I was living with grandmother from time to time. I thought, "Where can I go?" I decided to walk down the street and make a call on the old ring box phone in Mr. Crockett's Store. There it was, hanging on the wall just as I walked in. Over to my right was the most beautiful shiny telephone with bells and other strange parts. I requested to use the old phone and Mr. Crockett approved.

As I picked up the receiver and heard a click and the person said, "Information Please."

I wasn't sure what to say. I replied, "This is Wayne and I don't feel so good today."

She replied, "What is wrong? I'll do what I can to help you." Well, I replied, "I returned from school today and no one was home and I don't feel good."

Then she replied, "What did you eat for lunch today?" I explained to her "Grandmother fixed me a peanut butter sandwich, a cookie and an apple." Then "Information Please" said to me. "Is there anything else wrong?" I said, "Yes, I miss my grandmother and I sure miss my mother and I cry at night to see her."

"Information Please" was so kind and explained to me in a very soft voice. "Maybe what you need to do is return to grandmother's home and wait for her, as she may be close by and looking for you. Also, God is watching over you too, as He loves little children and remember what you learned in your Sunday School classes with all the flannel graph teachings."

Boy! "Information Please" sure understood my hurts and the way I felt. As I explained, "I'll return home and wait for grandmother." I thanked her, "Information Please" that is, and returned home thinking to myself, "Information Please" really does know a lot of things about little boys and girls like me. Maybe one day I'll be able to meet her wherever she is in that box.

Sure enough, grandmother was home and had just returned from Mrs. Henley's home with some eggs to make me a very tasty pie. She had a big smile on her face when I walked in and wasn't upset with me. I sure love my grandmother, and "Information Please" was right, God does keep His angels looking over us.

# Reflections

As we take our steps in life we never know what the next moment may be, or what impression we'll leave upon another as in the story "Information Please." We can't take life as just being another day, for we are here for a purpose. We come into this world fresh from the Master's hands. As pilgrims on a journey, our souls are searching and longing for the right path in love, goodness, peace, joy and happiness and the touch of other human beings.

So our purpose, as the little story above, there are other worlds and angels watching over us, and we must tell others about the other worlds and our God of all creation and his son Jesus Christ.

From the old telephone to the potbelly stove and sandbox as I've previously mentioned, to all the canned goods on the shelves behind the countertop, to all the display cases filled with beautiful fabrics, sewing notions and much, much more, what a wonderful store Mr. Crockett owned, and such a pleasant gentleman he always was.

Many years have passed since those unforgettable times of the forties in the Village of Cripple Creek. It seems as yesterday to me. Maybe we've lost some of the touch of time we can't buy with money. A time to relax from all of the days work and toil, a time to be in friendship and love for each other, sharing just good old fashion days of our lives.

by Wayne King

Painting by Nate Owens, National and International Artist

"Wrong Number," how did that happen? What happened to "Information Please?" All I wanted to do is call Cripple Creek, Virginia, the old Yonce Grocery Store at the Cripple Creek Mall. For goodness sakes, them people are so nice and I just wanted a little hog fat to chew on. Guess I sure messed up this time. Crazy cat ran away and I'm stuck with "Wrong Number."

# Doctor Andrew Bayne Grubb, a Visit to Grandmother's

Without question, Doctor Grubb was a very caring doctor in Cripple Creek and the surrounding area. As a young boy, I distinctly remember walking into Dr. Grubb's office one day when I was about eight or nine years old and with astonishment I observed shelves filled with beautiful bottles all labeled with their contents. I didn't fully know what was in the bottles or jars until sometime later.

It seemed Doctor Grubb never slept and was on call twenty four (24) hours a day, three hundred sixty five (365) days a year. He was the last of the old "Country Doctors" and always ready to call on anyone who needed him.

One summer while living with my grandmother I became ill and grandmother didn't know what was wrong with me. I had a high fever and was sweating like crazy. Grandmother immediately made her way to contact Dr. Grubb. He soon arrived. Checking me over, he looked at grandmother and wanted to know if she had any hog fat. She said "Yes." So Dr. Grubb ordered or prescribed the same for me to chew on the piece of hog fat and see if it would break the fever. It did. To this day I don't know or understand what the hog fat had to do with my fever, but it worked. Maybe one day I'll discover through the Foxfire books on home remedies just what happens in the human body when one chews hog fat.

Dr. Grubb's office was built in Cripple Creek, Virginia in 1910 and closed at his death in 1959.
Photo, postcard from Ruth Davidson.

Photo Courtesy of Hilda and Jim Grubb

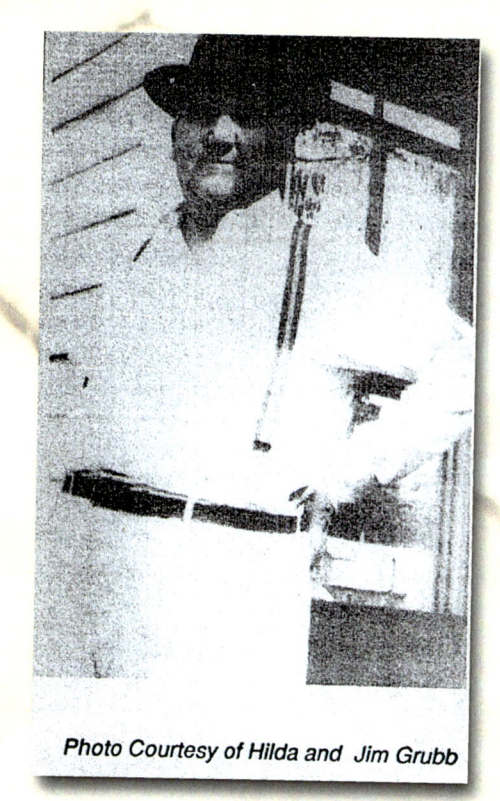

Dr. Andrew Bayne Grubb

Cripple Creek in the early 1900's
Dr. Andrew Bayne Grubb's office under construction in the upper right.
Photo provided by Clayta Bryant

## DR. ANDREW BAINE GRUBB

From the time Dr. Andrew Grubb came to Cripple Creek in July 1910 until his death, he served the people of Wythe and Grayson counties. He answered calls day and night, usually riding from place to place on the back of a horse. He often went unpaid for his duties.

# DR. ANDREW BAINE GRUBB

He'd come riding down the dirt roads of the county on a large rawboned horse with his supplies in saddle bags thrown across the horse's back. On cold days he wore a big old black bearskin coat.

"It made no difference how cold it was, how dark or how stormy, he would come," said Bill Groseclose, who grew up under Dr. Grubb's care. "When he'd see you, he'd walk over and feel of you and start telling some kind of old tale and you'd know you were going to be okay. But if he'd turn around, start whistling and have a frown on his face, you knew you were in trouble."

Bal was talking about Dr. Andrew Baine Grubb, one of many physicians who served Wythe County in the 1920s and 1930s. During that time most of the doctors made house calls and traveled many miles to help their patients.

Dr. Grubb came to Wythe County in July 1910 after graduating at the top of his class from the University College of Medicine in Richmond. He bought the house and practice of Dr. W. L. Slicer of Cripple Creek and worked the practice until his death in 1959. According to an article published in the ENTERPRISE at the time of Dr. Grubb's death, when he bought the practice he also received four cases of typhoid fever. It was only a few days after taking over these four cases that there were three more for the new doctor to care for. "He professionally served the seven for weeks with the fee for all the visits and medicine being a dollar bill," the article read.

When the name of Dr. Grubb is mentioned one image seems to come to the minds of those who knew him--a dedicated, unselfish doctor who truly cared about his patients. "He never asked you if you had the money or anything," said Ballard Groseclose, a life-time friend of Dr. Grubb. "He was a real humanitarian. He loved people and he loved to do things for them and he loved to help them. Money was not considered in his calls. If you didn't have the money, you still got the service."

Groseclose was just a small boy when Dr. Grubb came to Cripple Creek. His brother had shot his own toe off and the family called the doctor. That was the start of a long relationship between the two.

After Groseclose was married and had a family and home of his own, Dr. Grubb would come to his house to share many meals and to talk. The two families lived about five miles apart. He was also there whenever the family needed him. "One night he came in here and stood right there," Groseclose recalled. "He had on the old bearskin black overcoat and he'd got caught in a big snow blizzard. My kids were sick. I had two boys. And he said, "Bal, I couldn't go to sleep tonight 'til I come to see how your kids were." I put his horse in the barn and he stayed here a couple or three days, making his calls from here."

During this time the people in Cripple Creek had a party line telephone system they had gone together and put up. This was how families contacted Dr. Grubb and how he called to check on them. "We had an old party line phone on the wall and each person had a different ring," Grosecolse explained. "Some of them had a long, short and long, or three longs, or two shorts and a long. Dr. Grub would call home and say, "Hal, I,m at Bal's and everybody knew where he was if they needed him.

After several years of a close friendship, 'Bal' became the busy doctor's "nurse." "I didn't have any qualifications for being a nurse, but I would go with him and he would teach me. He would let me diagnose cases first then he would and say, 'Bal, you were exactly right. When he got older he would call me to go and see a patient to see if they were really sick before he came out.

The Groseclose family was not the only one in Wythe that came to love, respect and depend on Dr. Grubb. It is said that during his 49 years of practice in the rural areas of Wythe and Grayson counties he delivered close to 3,000 babies. He treated people with every known disease and was on the run literally with three epidemics of smallpox, and the polio epidemics of 1920 and 1950. He pulled teeth, removed bullets and appendixes.

Dr. Grubb had two cars during his years of practice. The first he purchased in 1912. It was a Saxon with a 15 horsepower motor. In the 1950's the people of Cripple Creek went together and purchased a car for the doctor who had helped them without asking for anything through the many years. Cars were often unfit for service over the rough country roads, across creeks, branches and through deep hollows.

Dr. Grubb's daughter-in-law, Hilda Grubb of Cripple Creek, said that his concern for a patient didn't end even after the patient went to a hospital and was under the care of another doctor. "When he sent patients to the hospital in Charlottesville, he would go on a train with them and stay until after their surgery, then come back and tell their families how they were doing. You always felt as soon as Pap walked in the door, everything was going to be all right."

Southwest Viriginia Enterprise, March 30, 1987

# A Sunrise Service

### Atop the mountain in

### Cripple Creek, Virginia

It's on the mountain top so let his praises ring!

Echoes of His Love overlooking meadows below of spring!

His Mercy brings life eternal, Christ Jesus has risen for all, let all who love Him, sing!

"Christ belongs to all people. He belongs to the whole world."

### Billy Graham

"If any man will come after me, let him deny himself, and take up his cross daily and follow me." Luke 9:23

# Sunrise Service in Cripple Creek

The old Methodist Church in Cripple always held a Sunrise Service each year atop the hill, in front of grandmother's home. It was a very steep climb, yet so many people climbed to the top as it was their first priority every Easter Sunday.

To see the elderly, ones with canes walking and sweating as they climbed a few steps at a time, knowing it would be hard, but rewarding when they reached the top. They had no chairs, no real place to sit except on the ground. The ground was hard and wet at times from a recent shower of rain. One thing for sure, there was reverence, respect and thankfulness in their hearts. People would bring blankets or an old pillow to rest on. It was truly a time to reflect spiritually and realize the power of God in their lives and to give Him praise and glory!

It was such a beautiful time to stand and see God's creation surrounding all the people and to know and think: our Lord Jesus Christ rose from the dead, giving us life and a hope within our hearts.

As the services proceeded with open prayer and thankfulness in mind and heart, there was a seeking the kingdom and His righteousness, a fullness of respect and reverence. An awesome stillness of the hour took place, and a slight breeze struck each face as a reminder to each person that it's God's creation and to know it's by grace we are all saved.

Painter's Home

"I will lift up mine eyes unto the hills, from whence cometh my help.
My help cometh from the Lord, which made heaven and earth."

Psalm 121:1-2 (KJV)

As the prayer was concluded and suddenly dawn broke forth, the sun's rays penetrated the open skies with splendor, a gorgeous appearance, a grandeur as though it could be a scene of possible likeness of the Lord's coming and lifting us into His radiant mercy and glory.

"Drop down ye heavens, from above, and let the skies pour down righteousness: let the earth open, and let them bring forth salvation, and let righteousness spring up together; I the Lord have created it."

Isaiah 45:8 (KJV)

After prayer, the congregation was addressed with a short sermon of appreciation for all the Lord had provided in His love and forgiveness and for His Son Jesus Christ and His resurrection.. Anyone not knowing our Lord was given an opportunity to accept Christ as their personal Savior.

"As far as the east is from the west, so far hath he removed our transgressions from us."

Psalm 103: 12 (KJV)

Upon receiving the Word of God, a request for prayer was opened before the congregation. Many would stand and be prayed for, waiting with expectations.

> "Give ear to my words, O Lord, consider my meditation. Hearken unto the voice of my cry, my king, and my God: for unto thee will I pray. My voice shalt thou hear in the morning, O Lord; in the morning will I direct my prayer unto thee, and will look up."
>
> Psalm 5:1-3 (KJV)

Once prayer was concluded, people would visit and gaze out upon the small village of Cripple Creek and the surrounding area. An astonishing scene of God's creation and beauty, hard to describe, yet so wonderful for the moment of time before them. The rolling hills and the beginning of Spring as the flowers and all of God's creation breaks forth. So apropos.

I've endeavored to give an account of what happened long ago, and pray I've depicted a close reflection of that precious hour.

# Slop Jars and Chamber Pots

Slop Jars and Chamber Pots…"WOW!" What are these things?

"No way, no way," she exclaimed, as our young daughter of eight years replied to her mother, my wife. "That thing stinks, I don't know what it is as it's made of metal, has a lid on it and I'll never use it; I may slip into it and never return…that slop jar you call it, no, no." She was not about to sit on this newly found object of discomfort. It even looked as though she might slip down into this thing and never get out as her body was very small for her age.

This was a humorous situation at the time for some of us, but not so humorous for our little daughter. None of our three children had ever been exposed to an outhouse, Chamber Pot or what grandmother called the Slop Jar or any of the primitive ways grandmother lived in the little Village of Cripple Creek. Grandmother had always placed the old Slop Jar in a small closet just outside the kitchen for use during the night in case one needed immediate relief. A Sears and Roebuck Catalog was always within reach…those shiny pages…well you know. The closet was built on a screened-in-porch which helped especially during the cold winter months.

Our trip was an exciting one and the experience was one never to be replaced or forgotten…not to mention the old straw tick mattress and chicken feather pillows we used.

Now that you know the story, the question is, "Would you use the old Chamber Pot or the so called Slop Jar?"

Slop Jar, thanks to my Uncle Kesiter King

# The Old Springhouse

Next door to my grandmother, lived Mrs. Laura Counselman. She had a wonderful way of keeping her food items cool without a refrigerator. Behind her home was a small building called a springhouse, completely sealed (except for a small door) and inside she had an artesian spring bubbling up with the freshest water ever. The water was very cold as it bubbled up from the ground forming a small pool. As one entered the small building you were required to shut the door behind you. Keeping things cold was very important because many times meat and dairy products were left in the small structure.

Mrs. Counselman not only used the springhouse for cooling dairy products and meat, but she had storage bins for potatoes, onions and other vegetables as needed. The old springhouse was used for anything requiring coolness.

There were times when Mrs. Counselman would invite me inside her home and if it happened to be winter months, we would sit in front of the fireplace and talk about the simple things of life. Our conversations may be about a beautiful bird, or a deer we saw in the nearby area…or about the weather and all the snow…just simple things. At other times, we would sit and listen to the fire in the fireplace while we rocked in the old rocking chairs being still and smiling once in awhile. Silence is a good teacher, yet knowing much of what the other person is thinking without a word said.

I miss the old days gone by when people weren't in such a hurry to go some place, and no need to really be there in the first place. One thing for sure, I always enjoyed Mrs. Counselman's company and her special way of showing her friendship. I really miss her.

Mrs. Laura Counselman's Home

# Cripple Creek's U.S. Post Office

As I've stated in one of my previous stories, going to the U.S. Post Office was an exciting time for me. I always enjoyed being able to make the tumblers in the mailbox work and find grandmother's box with mail inside. Back in those days it was a very exciting thing to have a letter in the mailbox. So few people wrote each other and many times it was the expense even though it cost pennies to mail a letter in days just after World War II.

Today, there isn't a post office in Cripple Creek, Virginia. According to a wonderful couple, Mr. and Mrs. Edward Yonce (owners of the post office building) confirmed Mr. C. Bayne Grubb's message, Cripple Creek Post Office closed January 10, 2008 after one hundred and ten years (110) of operation. The post office was officially closed and items removed thereafter. So many wonderful people passed through the doors of the old post office and the yesterday's are long gone but not forgotten as the memories are still lodged in the corners of my mind forever and so pleasant they remain.

What a surprise to learn from Mr. and Mrs. Yonce, they are sending one of the original brass mailbox doors or faces, with the old fashion combination lock. What a beautiful face it has with the relief of the American Bald Eagle. How fascinating to think I might have even touched this old mailbox face at some point when I was a young boy. Now I might be able to construct a mailbox with the beautiful door and use it to tell my story to other young children.

Recently I discovered an address in a Bible given to me by my mother, Francis Juanita King March 4, 1945 in Cripple Creek, Virginia. My address was, Post Office Box 6, Cripple Creek, Virginia. Mrs. Yonce explained to me by phone, box 6 was a general delivery number for my mail at that time. My, how times have changed.

**THE CRIPPLE CREEK GROCERY:** The last class four U.S. post office in the county is located in the center of downtown Cripple Creek. It's known locally as the "Cripple Creek Mall."

Photo courtesy of Wytheville Enterprises

Recent photo of the Cripple Creek Post Office
Courtesy of Mr. Eddie Yonce

Mr. Eddie Yonce reaching out to help anyone. His last and closing days in the old Cripple Creek Post Office. As stated in the Wytheville Enterprise Newspaper, his hand and his wife's hand was always reaching out to help the community in anyway possible.

The above courtesy has always been a reflection of those living in Cripple Creek over many, many decades. Yes, it was a sad day to see the old U.S. Post Office close its door with no more letters, packages and special orders of whatever it may have been.

(Cripple Creek Postmaster January 8, 2008)

Jean Farley

**MAIL MAN:** Eddie Yonce retired from his position as Cripple Creek's postmaster on Thursday after 36 years on the job. Although he will continue to operate the adjoining Cripple Creek Grocery, the post office will close on Jan. 11.

**By NATE HUBBARD**/Staff

For the first time in 36 years, Eddie Yonce woke up on Friday with only one job.
Yonce, 63, who has served the dual roles as Cripple Creek postmaster and store owner for nearly four decades, retired Thursday from the U.S. Postal Service.
The end of Yonce's career also marks the end of the 110-year history of Cripple Creek's post office as the operation is scheduled to shut down on Jan. 11.
"You hate to see a community lose anything, but as far as the mail service of the people they'll still receive mail service on a rural route," Yonce said.
In the interim eight days between Yonce's retirement and the closure of the post office, Yonce's wife, Frances, will take care of the postal duties.
"My wife is my postmaster relief," Eddie said.
That Frances will help close down the post office is fitting as it was Frances who first brought Eddie to Cripple Creek.
Eddie was born near Rural Retreat and grew up in Wytheville before his marriage to Frances brought him farther south in Wythe County.
He took on the postmaster role a few years after his move to Cripple Creek when he bought the grocery store and accompanying post office property from the previous owner. Nobody else applied for the postmaster position so the job was his.
"When I first started I think the salary on this office was about $4,400 a year so you couldn't make a living on it alone," Eddie said. "You had to have a business or something to go along with it."
He said the store and post office mutually assisted each other.
"The business and the post office working together, they each benefit one another," he said. "A person comes in to get their mail, they pick up things in the store; they come in the store to get things, a lot of times they'll buy money orders, they'll buy a book of stamps or whatever they need out of the post office. They work real good together."
Although the post office portion of their business is shutting down, Eddie and Frances still will continue to operate Cripple Creek Grocery for the foreseeable future.
Postal service retirement thus won't mean relaxation for Eddie or a fade away from the Cripple Creek community.
"I'm going to keep the business going so I'll still have plenty to do," he said. "I won't have to worry about that."
Jim Crockett of Cripple Creek said Eddie always offered great service to the community during his 36 years as postmaster.
He mentioned Eddie's helpfulness, for example in keeping mail organized for people while they were on vacation, and his friendly demeanor.
"Eddie's a fine feller," Crockett said. "Eddie would help anybody out or do anything for him."

The long-time postmaster said the most difficult part of giving up the job will be losing the additional contact he had with customers from the mail room.

"Probably what I'll miss most about the job is the contact with the public, the people," Eddie said.

In his 36 years of service, Eddie saw a number of changes to the mail delivery industry. Stamps are about five times more expensive than they were in the early 1970s, and computers have changed the nature of the business.

Eddie pointed to the influx of computer technology as one of the hardest challenges he faced during his postmaster career.

"When I came through high school we were not trained on computers so I had to pick up all of this," Eddie said. "Some of the other postmasters helped me in getting trained for the computers and all and that was probably one of the more challenging things that I've had since I've been in the postal service."

The Cripple Creek community also has changed as the population has aged and retired. Eddie said when he first started many Cripple Creek residents worked in jobs that took them away from the area for most of the week, making P.O. boxes an attractive option. Many of those residents have since retired and shifted their mail service to a mailbox in front of their home. At one point he said about 55 of Cripple Creek's 100 families rented a P.O. box, but that number had dwindled to about half that total when Eddie started telling people in late 2007 of the post office's closing upon his forthcoming retirement.

Despite the postmaster job generally being one of routine and organization, Eddie said he's seen a few odd things come through his mail room.

"Probably one of the things that a lot of people don't realize that is shipped in the mail, people can buy honeybees in the mail," he said. "They come in a cage, they're screened in a cage the whole swarm of bees, and I've never had any problem with it, but if something ever happened to damage that and the bees got out, you've got problems."

He said he remembered one Cripple Creek resident whose shipment of bees arrived with the bees all dead – but that still was a better situation than having a swarm of bees getting loose in his office.

On his final day as postmaster last week, Eddie exuded pride in the organization he has been an employee of for 36 years.

As an avid stamp collector, he marveled at the price rare stamps can command at auctions. But most of all he said he was struck by the amazing efficiency of the postal service that most people might not stop to think about.

"You take the U.S. Postal Service, you can compare it to any postal service there is in the entire world, there is none that comes close to being as efficient as the U.S. Postal Service," he said. "They're the most efficient of any of them and for the distance you can send a letter they're the cheapest."

Nate Hubbard can be reached at 228-6611 or nhubbard@wythenews.com.

(Post Office Closing Sidebar January 8, 2008)

By **NATE HUBBARD**/Staff

Although Eddie Yonce's retirement as postmaster is bringing an end to a century-long tradition of brick-and-mortar postal service in Cripple Creek, residents of the area shouldn't see a substantial change in their available mail services.
The most significant change is the elimination of P.O. boxes in Cripple Creek. Yonce, however, said that many residents had already made the shift to rural route mailboxes in front of their homes even before he announced the post office would be closing after his retirement.
During the last two months, Yonce said he has been working to get people set up with personal mailboxes. As of his retirement date on Thursday, he said that only about a half dozen P.O. boxes remained rented at the Cripple Creek post office.
Jim Crockett was one P.O. box renter who has been affected by the looming post office closure. Crockett said he had been going to the Cripple Creek post office for about 40 years and liked having a P.O. box for the convenience of being able to get his mail when he stopped by the neighboring Cripple Creek Grocery that Yonce also owns.
In late November, Crockett made the switch to a mailbox in front of his property.
While most residents already have made the transition to a home mailbox, P.O. box options still will remain at post offices in neighboring communities.
Kim Mangus, Speedwell postmaster and part of the U.S. Postal Service team that is assisting in the transition coming about from Cripple Creek's closure, said she has plenty of room at her post office for any Cripple Creek residents who still want a P.O. box.
"We're actually talking about expanding my office," she said.
The Speedwell and Ivanhoe post offices are each less than 10 miles from Cripple Creek.
In addition, Yonce said mail carriers are able to provide many of the services that a post office can offer.
"The only advantage to a post office is that you can go to a post office anytime during the day that it's open and if you need to talk to the rural carrier you have to be there when he runs," Yonce said.
Carriers can sell stamps and even can provide money orders, although as Yonce mentioned, the turnaround time is slower because the carrier has to pick up the payment one day before providing the money order the next time the route is run.
The ability of computers to provide automated postal services also can help mitigate the loss of the physical store – although the rise of computer technology also was one of the factors in the Cripple Creek post office's closure.
"What it boils down to is efficiency," said David Walton, a USPS spokesperson for the Appalachian district. "More and more transactions are starting to move out of lobbies because of usps.com."
Mangus also mentioned the possibility that the postal service will install a cluster of mailboxes near the Cripple Creek post office site that would allow P.O. box renters to retrieve their mail close to their familiar location.
Many decisions like the cluster of mailboxes option, though, are still undecided.
"A lot of things are still up in the air," Mangus said. "Nothing is set in stone."

Walton said he wouldn't go as far as saying that closing down small post offices is becoming a trend, but he again emphasized the wide range of services available at www.usps.com.

Although Crockett has made a smooth transition to a mailbox on a rural route, he said he's still concerned about the loss of identity for Cripple Creek with the loss of its post office.

"I don't want an Ivanhoe address and I don't want a Speedwell address," he said.

Despite the post office's scheduled closure on Jan. 11, Walton said officially Cripple Creek is only having its services suspended.

A formal closure has to be made by the postal rate commission with public hearings and that process would not take place for a few years, Walton added.

"The name stays on the books at least for a couple years," he said.

Even if in the future the rate commission did officially eliminate the Cripple Creek postal designation, Walton said that decision would only affect the area's zip code.

"They can keep the Cripple Creek address line," he said, adding that he understood the importance of a community keeping its identity through the use of its name. "They would just have a new zip code."

Although the postal service has a long history in Cripple Creek, Yonce said the physical location of the post office actually has moved multiple times in its 110 years.

Yonce said the community's post office is classified as fourth class, meaning that the postmaster has to furnish the building for the office. That requirement led to the location shifting from business to business in the area as the postmaster job changed hands.

By the end of the week, though, the old white sign showing the post office's current and final Cripple Creek location will be nothing more than a memento.

"I'll keep it as a souvenir," Yonce said.

Nate Hubbard can be reached at 228-6611 or nhubbard@wythenews.com.

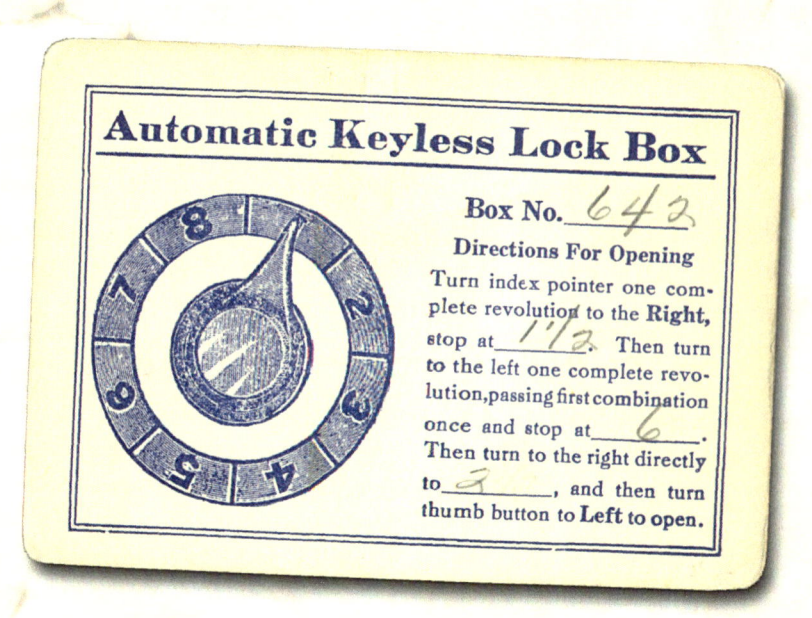

Automatic Keyless Lock Box combination card.

Last postcard stamped from the Cripple Creek Post Office January 11, 2008.

A sad day indeed…

Post Office Box 642

Original Post Office Mailbox Door, Cripple Creek, Virginia

Courtesy of Mr. and Mrs. Eddie Yonce

Cripple Creek Grocery and U.S. Post Office
Please note "Old Glory"
January 1993

# Post Office Department
## FOURTH ASSISTANT POSTMASTER GENERAL
### Washington

6/20/10

Sir:
In order that this office may determine, with as much accuracy as possible, the relative positions of Post Offices, so that they may be correctly delineated on its maps, please carefully answer the questions below, and furnish the diagram on the other side, returning the same as soon as possible, verified by your signature and dated.

Respectfully,

_____
Fourth Assistant Postmaster General.

To Postmaster at _Cripple Creek,_
_Wythe Co.,_
_Va._

The (P. O. Dept.) name of my Office is _Cripple Creek, Va._

If the town, village, or site of the Post Office be known by another name than that of the Post Office, state that other name here: _____

My Office is situated in _____ part of _____ Township, or in _____ quarter of Tract No. _____, _____ Township, County of _____ State of _____

- The name of the most prominent ~~river~~ CREEK near it is _Cripple Creek_
- The name of the nearest creek is _Francis Mill Creek_
- My Office is _64 Rods_ miles from said ~~river~~ creek, on the _South_ side of it, and is _2 Rods_ ~~miles~~ from said nearest creek, on the _West_ side of it.
- My Office is on Mail Route No. _____
- My Office is a Special Office supplied from _____, _____ miles distant.
- The name of the nearest Office on my route is _____, and its distance is _____ miles, by the traveled road, in a _____ direction from this, my Office.
- The name of the nearest Office, on the same route, on the other side, is _____ and its distance is _____ miles in a _____ direction from this, my Office.
- The name of the nearest Office off the route is _____, and its distance by the most direct road is _____ miles in a _____ direction from this, my Office.
- My Office is at a distance of _6.2 Rods_ from the track of the _N&W_ Railroad, on the _South_ side of the railroad.
- My Office is _3_ miles, air-line distance, from nearest point of my County boundary.

(Signature of Postmaster) _David A. Moore_

(Date) JUN 23 1910

Application to Post Office Department, Washington D.C., June 23, 1910

By David A. Moore Post Master, Cripple Creek, Virginia

Photo Copy by Mrs. Francis Yonce

Early Pictures of the Cripple Creek Post Office

Photo courtesy of Mrs. Pearl C. Woods

**Post Office and Claude Moore's Store**

Photo courtesy of Mrs. Daphne Rosenbaum

Photo Courtesy of Peal C. Woods

**EVERYTHING UNDER THE SUN:** Francis Yonce runs the counter at the Cripple Creek Grocery in downtown Cripple Creek while her husband, Edward, operates the post office in the next room. The little store sells most anything you could want, and if you don't see it, you can just ask. For a better look at the country stores of central Wythe County see page B1 for additional photographs.

Mrs. Yonce reaching out to help someone with their list of items for the day. Just another example of the courtesy one will find in the little village of Cripple Creek...reminding me of the days when I lived there and was helped by the Crockett family over sixty years ago. What a blessing to see special attention continuing year after year with the love for those who have chosen to help others.

# A closing note:

I apologize for not having an inside picture of the U.S. Post Office in Cripple Creek, but here is an example of what they once looked like so many years ago. My wife is ready to get her mail…not really. This office was closed many years ago and the building destroyed .

Pictures taken in Pistol River, Oregon in 1992

157

# Grandmother King and a Buried Treasure

(Spanish Mill Coin 1784)

Many years ago in the early nineteen sixties, my grandmother Minnie King, wrote and sent a letter to my wife and I stating a short story about a black man who owed her some money for items he purchased from her little grocery store in Virginia.

This account doesn't relate directly to Cripple Creek but did occur in another rural area some distance from Cripple Creek. As grandmother King explained. A black man in the nearby area had an account with her for staples he purchased. It was always the custom or policy to settle accounts on time and keep good credit. Usually a running list was just fine without too many details…just put it on the tab.

One day the gentleman owing grandmother money walked into her little store and told her he was plowing with his mule in a near by area and the old bull plow struck an object in the ground and when he looked down, it was an old ceramic crock filled with silver coins. What a find and how many coins he discovered I was never told. He proceeded to ask grandmother King if she would be willing to take one silver coin for each dollar he owed her for his debt? Grandmother explained she would and later was told the gentleman went into town and paid the banker in silver for another debt he owed.

To this day I don't know the full story, but what a wonderful find it was. Grandmother sent a silver coin to each grandchild, as she explained and the one I received was one of America's first silver dollars known as the Spanish Mill. These coins were used among the 13 colonies' and very popular. My coin is dated 1784, CAROLUS 8 III, DEI GRATIA (front), HISPAN.etind.REX.m.8R.F.M. (back).

Thomas Jefferson recommended that they become official legal tender of the United States. The Spanish Mill coins were the forerunners of the first U.S. silver dollar minted in 1794.

Please see the picture of my coin below.

Mrs. Minnie Lou King (My grandmother) and Jimmy King's (My uncle) children, Timothy King, Diane King, Linda Gail King, and Michael King. Grandmother's grocery store in background.

My grandmother, Minnie Lou King
Age 65, 1958

Mom Dad & Dillard

Mr. and Mrs. James Henry King and son,
Morris Dillard King my father.

Picture taken in about 1918 or 1919.

162

# Hands In The Cookie Jar

O' little hands in the cookie jar: So many goodies baked with love and tender care, thinking of you.

O' little hands in the cookie jar: Expressions of happiness and smiles that never fade away, special and true.

Hands in the cookie jar: All day long.
Hands in the cookie jar: I'll sing you a song.
Hands in the cookie jar: God's love to you all day long.
Hands in the cookie jar: I'll give you a smile.
Hands in the cookie jar: Shows acts of love longer than a mile.
Hands in the cookie jar: Hot and sweet, smelling great just for you!
Hands in the cookie jar: Mixed with raisins, nuts, candies, sugar and a little flour will do.
Hands in the cookie jar: So soft and tender, designed especially for you.
Hands in the cookie jar: I'll spend time with you.
Hands in the cookie jar: Will make you strong all night through.
Hands in the cookie jar: I'll always make more, special and true, just for your love, I see in you.
Hands in the cookie jar: Just one more time.
Hands in the cookie jar: You'll always find Jesus in me, loving you!

Just like my grandmother in Cripple Creek, Virginia. My wife Hattie King, always enjoys baking cookies for everyone. She is one fantastic cook… Hattie's Cookies, Yum, Yum!

Hattie's 70th birthday.. our friends and Christian family, left to right, Jeremiah, Dusty, Jessica, Joseph and little Jonathon Armstrong.

164

# Hattie's Kitchen

In Hattie's Kitchen no other will do. Her love is flowing just for you.

Early in the morning she starts her day with God's love to bake the best cookies directed from heaven above.

Scurrying from space to space, she is looking for the very best ingredients to mix for you and your special taste.

Bowls, spoons, forks, utensils sure, an electric mixer will surely help her through.

The oven is on so hot and blue, the heat will bake those cookies through and through.

The time is right as she mixes with vigor, two thirds cup of soft shortening (part butter), one half cup granulated sugar, one half cup of brown sugar (packed), never over do, one egg, and a little vanilla, one teaspoon for you, now stir together and blend, to make it ever so true … until the mixture thickens, especially for you.

Now sift together and stir in one and a half cups sifted GOLD MEDAL Flour, one half teaspoon of soda, no more will do. For the final touch, one-half teaspoon of salt and one-half cup of chopped nuts and a six ounce package of semi-sweet chocolate pieces (about one and a forth cups) will bring smiles, all for you.

Time to pull out the cookie sheets, first one, then two, then three, yes one more all well greased will do. Pressed on the cookie sheets, one and two, until all the dough is gone on all four, ready for your smiles, all will calm you.

Finally, the oven is set at 375 degrees, cookies are baking (eight to ten minutes) and the aroma is flowing throughout the house as she sings a little song for you. Cookies, cookies bake so fast until golden brown, melting in your mouth in just a flash.

So, if you want the best cookies all the time, taste and eat in Hattie's Kitchen next time. She is filled with love from heaven above, be careful, don't drop a single cookie on the rug.

   Always remember, Jesus is there in all the corners you see, just waiting for praise from you and me.

Hattie's cookies, so rich and fine, so watch out where you dine!

   Hard times or good times. One thing for sure, my wife Hattie is so much like her mother and grandmother (Hattie) when it comes to cooking. She can always do with very little to meet the needs of all and serve them with the most delicious meal in town…just like grandmother in Cripple Creek.

   She understands how to take out the old kettles, pots and pans and firing up the old wood stove to meet all the family demands…enough food for an army.

Hattie King, my wife
April 1992

# Are All the Children In?

I think ofttimes as night draws nigh

Of an old house on a hill,

Of a yard all wide and blossom starred

Where children played at will

And when night at last came down,

Hushing the merry din,

Mother would look around and ask,

"Are all the children in?"

Tis many a year since then,

And the old house on the hill

No longer echoes to childish feet,

And the yard is still, so still,

But I see it all as shadows creep,

And though many the years have been,

Even now, I am hearing my mother ask,

"Are all the children in?"

I wonder if when the shadows fall

On the last day short, earthly day;

When we say good-by to the world outside,

All tired with our childish play;

When we step out into the Other Land

Where mother so long has been,

Will we hear her ask, as we did of old,

"Are all the children in?"

And I wonder, too, what the Lord will say

To us older children of His;

Have we cared for the lambs and shown them the fold?

A privilege joyful it is.

And I wonder, too, what our answers will be

When His loving questions begin:

"Have you brought the children in?"


(Author Unknown)

# There is a Real Change In Cripple Creek

Seems the old buggy has long taken its place in some river along with all the old Model "T" and all of its predecessors.

Change has taken place in Cripple Creek with a mobile jail and a neighborhood watch to help keep the peace. One never knows when the authorities are needed to arrest those who chase out of season deer from the mountains for an evening meal. There is always ample room in the public jailhouse, but keep in mind for a jailhouse lawyer.

Close to home…Thanks to Mrs. Daphne Rosenbaum.

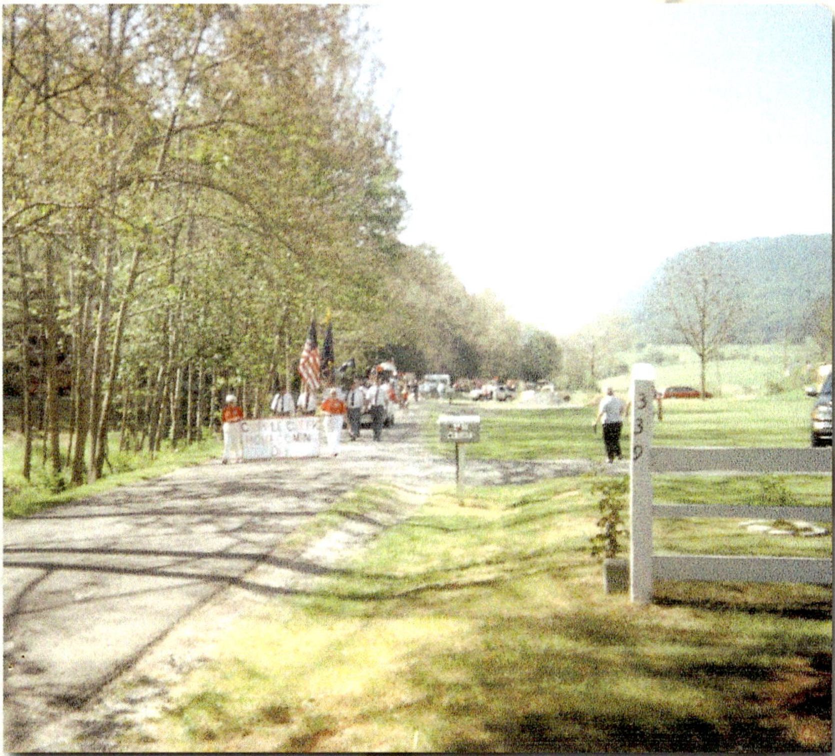
339

# The Old Water Pump

Believe it or not, the old water pump I once used at my grandmother's in Cripple Creek is still working. I can't image after all these years dating back to the 1940's, she still brings up the precious liquid. I've pumped hundreds of gallons of water for grandmother's use in her home and plenty for the chickens and cows.

Mr. Rosenbaum (present owner of my grandmother's property) was kind enough to send me a recent picture of the old water pump and even pumped some water up for me to see. Thank you Mr. Rosenbaum.

# Forever Giving--Forever Living

"Every valley shall be filled, and every mountain and hill shall be brought low;   and the crooked shall be made straight, and the rough ways shall be made smooth;   And all flesh shall see the salvation of God."

Luke 3:5-6 (KJV)

O' Lord my God, I search for you, my soul longs to be with you.  I look into the heavens above as I walk in the fields of the daffodils; their warm yellow color sends calming over my soul, for the creation of your beauty has grasped me.  My heart spins as a lily of the pond, your love is beyond the crimson red of the rose.  May I know your rhythm and find forgiveness as you remember my wrongs no more and forget them forever more.  You clothe me with your mercy and cause my soul to flood over the banks as rain falls from a cloud and fills the valleys below causing rivers to break forth over their banks.

O' Lord my God, may virtue be my call, and unto you may I sing to you as a bird in the air, for you are my love and all beauty you have created is far beyond  the comprehension of man.  Let me find you in my heart, in my soul, and my spirit filled with your love, forever giving, forever living.

Wayne King

# Time to Say Good-Bye to Old Cripple Creek

Well, when we say good-by in the old English, the contraction, "God go with you," is a wonderful way in sending a blessing as we close the few short stories about Cripple Creek and a few other areas in Virginia.

Departing from my grandparent's old home place to another adventure somewhere in some place, to experience another time in space of happiness, more moments of love, kindness and expressions of being able to remember treasured memories deep within the corners of one's mind. I've missed those days of long ago and it's hard to depart from them. Only from the mind of yesterday will I play forever the sounds of trickling water flowing over the rocks in the old Francis Mill Creek as I lie on the old straw tick mattress and feather pillow as the mountain breezes carry the echoes of the beautiful surroundings of Cripple Creek. Maybe one day I'll return and look for some of the past to see if there lingers any touch of my childhood of so long ago.

# In Loving Memory of Keister Troy King

Uncle Keister was very special to Hattie, my wife and I and always displayed a happy face with love and compassion. He wanted so much to see this book completed before his untimely passing.

Even though his address has changed, we'll see him again one day because he gave his personal testimony to us and acceptance of our Lord and Savior Jesus Christ.

Yes, we see the horizon of life and know there is another shore ready to receive those who have gone ahead of us. His love will never be forgotten, as his actions always spoke louder than words.

We'll miss him for now, but never forgotten.

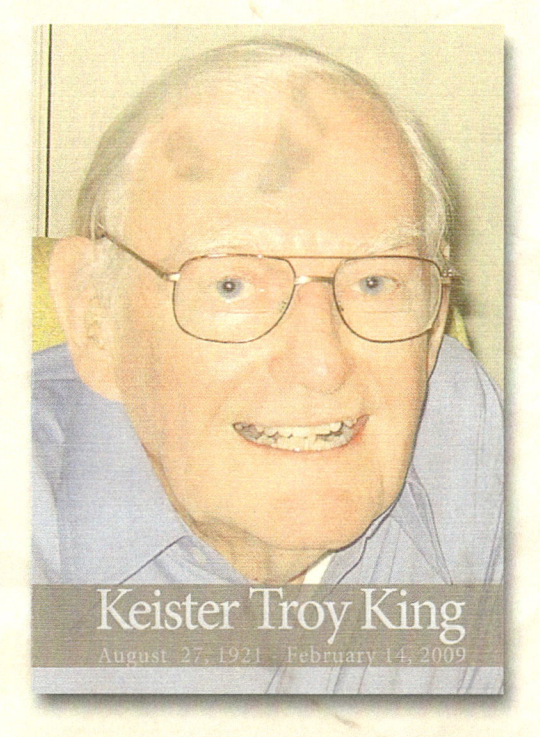

Keister Troy King
August 27, 1921 - February 14, 2009

# Celebration of Life

**The Pontoon Boat**

A Tribute to Keister Troy King
(Adopted from the Sailing Ship by Henry Van Dyke)

We are standing on the dock on Long Creek.
A small pontoon boat glides in the morning breeze and
starts for the ocean.
It is an object of beauty, and we stand watching it.
Till at last it passes under the bridge,
into the ocean and fades on the horizon.
Someone at my side says:
"He is gone."

Gone! Where?
Gone from our sight-that is all.
The boat is as real as it was when it left.
And just as able to bear her load of living freight to
its destination.
The diminished size and total loss of sight is in us.
not in it.

And just at the moment when someone at my side says,
"He is gone,"
There are others who are watching for him coming,
and other voices take up a glad shout:
"There he comes."

- and that is dying. A horizon and just the limit of
our sight.
Lift us up, Oh Lord, that we may see further.

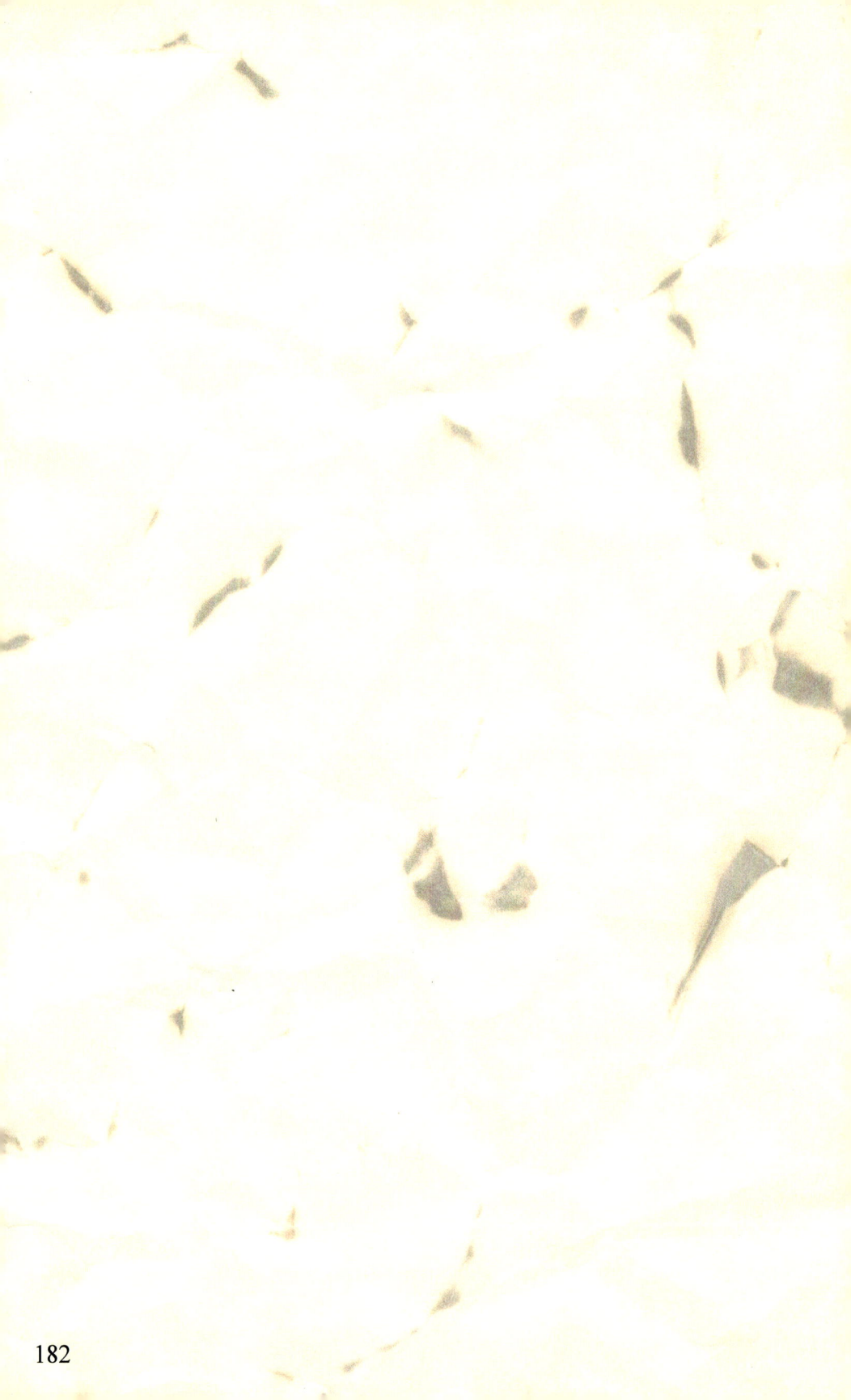